Paul's letter to the Galatians
A Devotional Commentary

M J Flower

The St Giles Commentary Series

Grosvenor House
Publishing Limited

All rights reserved
Copyright © M J Flower, 2024

The right of M J Flower to be identified as the author of this
work has been asserted in accordance with Section 78
of the Copyright, Designs and Patents Act 1988

The book cover is copyright to M J Flower

This book is published by
Grosvenor House Publishing Ltd
Link House
140 The Broadway, Tolworth, Surrey, KT6 7HT.
www.grosvenorhousepublishing.co.uk

This book is sold subject to the conditions that it shall not, by way of
trade or otherwise, be lent, resold, hired out or otherwise circulated
without the author's or publisher's prior consent in any form of
binding or cover other than that in which it is published and
without a similar condition including this condition being
imposed on the subsequent purchaser.

A CIP record for this book
is available from the British Library

ISBN 978-1-80381-695-1

Dedicated to
Margaret, David, Dorothy and John.

CONTENTS

About the Author   vii

Introduction   ix

Chapter 1   1

Chapter 2   29

Chapter 3   55

Chapter 4   79

Chapter 5   99

Chapter 6   139

Select Bibliography   149

About the Author

M J Flower, BA (Hons); MPhil, raised a family before reading Theology and Philosophy of Religion at the University of Exeter, where she also completed a research thesis on the social theory of John Millbank. She jointly established the Institute for Christian Studies in Exeter, and worked extensively with the South West Training Ministry for the Diocese of Exeter, training and supporting Readers and non-ordained ministers. She spent many years as a Churchwarden at St Leonard's Church in Exeter, and sat on the Deanery Synod as a lay member. She has spent more years than she would like to count leading and contributing to Bible Study and Home Groups and continues this work while happily retired in Buckinghamshire, living close to a very wide circle of friends and three generations of her family.

She is the author of *The King and the Kingdom: A devotional commentary on the Gospel of Matthew* and *The Acts of The Apostles: a devotional commentary*.

Introduction

Paul, an apostle, not from men nor through men, but through Jesus Christ and God the Father who raised him from the dead. And all the brethren who are with me.

To the churches of Galatia. Grace to you and peace from God the Father and the Lord Jesus Christ; who gave Himself for our sins, to deliver us from the present evil age according to the will of our God and Father;

To whom be glory for ever and ever. Amen.

Paul wrote letters. He did not write theological treatises or interpretations of sacred writings. He wrote to his friends, to his brothers and sisters in Christ, sometimes to encourage them, sometimes to inform them, sometimes to warn them of some specific danger to their life of faith. He speaks of himself in all humility as a sinner, as in 1 Timothy 1:15, but also as an apostle of Jesus Christ. In his letters we can see, though dimly, the kind of father in Christ he was to many of those who had first heard the gospel under his ministry. In his letters he tells them of his prayer for them, he thanks God for them, he sends special greetings to many of them. The letters are full of his love for them, even when they have gone astray.

Though when we read these letters we know that they were intended for people whose culture was different from our own, living in different situations and with different needs; yet because Paul lived under the anointing of the eternal and ever present Holy Spirit, his letters speak to us too. We have the privilege of holding these precious documents in our hands, documents which have become as important to us as they were to those who first read them.

Galatians Chapter 1

Galatians 1:2-5. The recipients of the letter to the Galatians

Paul first addresses the churches of Galatia with the blessing of 'grace and peace from God the Father and the Lord Jesus Christ', reminding them of the tremendous thing that has happened to them. They have come into the good of what the Lord Jesus Christ has done for them, giving Himself for their sins to deliver them from this present evil age, according to the will of their God and Father. (Galatians 1:3-5).

But this letter to the Galatians is no saccharine comfort zone. Paul is writing polemically with white hot indignation, for there are some in the churches of Galatia who are preaching 'another' gospel, which is not the true gospel. (Galatians 1:7).

It was an urgent situation, compromising the very foundation of the gospel of Christ; and a threat to their very existence as free men and women who were no longer under law but under grace, a 'different gospel' (Galatians 1:6) which would deny them the freedom with which Christ had made them free.

The Galatians to whom Paul's letter was written were the Christians of Pisidian Antioch; Iconium, Lystra, and Derbe. Galatia was a region of Asia Minor, and could be described as North and South Galatia. Historically, the inhabitants of Galatia were descended from an earlier Gaulish or Celtic tribe, but this tribe inhabited far more than the territory known as Galatia.

It has been hypothesised that Paul was writing to Galatia as a whole and not exclusively to the southern Galatia of Pisidian Antioch; Iconium, Lystra and Derbe. It is accepted that Paul could have been writing within the limits of the whole Galatian territory but more likely that his concern would be with those churches of south Galatia planted by him and Barnabas during the first missionary journey. (Acts 13:14-14:26). The question arises, why would Paul write to an area of north Galatia with which he had no connection?

It is true that he wrote to the Roman believers before he had been to Rome, but that letter was personal and included writing to and about people whom he knew. (Romans 16:1-23). There may of course have been 'churches of Galatia' within the extreme limits of the province, and churches in the north may have been included in this letter. If this is so, the heresy with which Paul is concerned in this letter may have spread even further and affected many more people, struggling between their loyalty to the gospel through which they had been brought to faith in Christ, and their loyalty to their former way of life.

Paul's concern was with all who had been 'called into the grace of Christ' through his preaching, (Galatians 1:6-10), though the Acts of the Apostles clearly defines Paul's ministry to south Galatia, and makes no mention of another journey to the north. From the contents of the letter it is evident that the threat of heresy was very real, and it is in response to this that Paul writes to the Galatians.

Galatians 1:1. The apostleship of Paul

Paul, an apostle - not from men, nor through men but through Jesus Christ and God the Father who raised Him from the dead - and all the brethren who are with me. To the churches of Galatia.

Grace to you and peace from God the Father and the Lord Jesus Christ who gave Himself for our sins to deliver us from the present evil age according to the will of our God and Father; to whom be glory for ever. Amen. (Galatians 1:1-5).

In Acts 9:15, Paul is described as a chosen vessel to the Lord, to bear His Name before the Gentiles and to have been set apart for this very purpose. (Galatians 1:1; Romans 1:1). When Paul introduces himself as an apostle, he is claiming that he is one who is 'sent', sent of course by God, one who has received a special commission from God.

Paul knew that there were other apostles equally commissioned, those who had been disciples of the Lord Jesus during His earthly ministry, the 'twelve' who had been apostles before him. Paul was not one of the twelve, and he knew he was not worthy to be called an apostle because he had persecuted the church of God. (1 Corinthians 15:9). But nevertheless, he was called 'by the will of God' to be an apostle of Jesus Christ. (1 Corinthians 1:10). His apostolic commission was not derived from men, through a human intermediary. It was received 'through Jesus Christ and God the Father'. (Galatians 1:1). This meant that he was not responsible to any human agency, but only to God the Father.

The Fatherhood of God was a declaration of Paul's adoption as a son into the family of God, the one whom he could call 'Abba, Father'. (Galatians 4:7; Romans 8:15; 16,21). Paul longed to know more and more of the power and authority of the Fatherhood of God in his life, that which Paul understood as the power which raised the Lord Jesus from the dead to the throne in heaven, the Resurrected Christ who appeared to him on the Damascus road. That appearance of Jesus to him was grace indeed. That was when he received the call upon his life, his commission to be an apostle, one sent not only to the sons of Israel but also to the Gentile world. (Acts 9:15; 26:17)

In his later letters, Paul recognizes others who are also 'messengers of Christ', apostles, like Titus and Apollos. (2 Corinthians 8:33; 1 Corinthians 4:6,9). In Galatians he is emphasizing his own apostleship because the Galatian believers need to understand that what he is writing to them carries the authority of God. There is a certain opposition to his apostleship, those who have reservations about his teaching, and do not accept that what he is warning them about so strongly, is absolutely fundamental to the gospel.

It appears from verse 1 that there were opponents of Paul who did not accept his authority as an apostle. Perhaps they maintained that he had received what authority he claimed to possess through some kind of authorization from the apostles in the Jerusalem church, the church to which Paul had gone twice. (Galatians 1:18; 2:1). Or that he may have received authorization from the church in Antioch of Syria, who after prayer and fasting had commissioned Paul and Barnabas to the work to which the Holy Spirit had called them. (Acts 13:2,3). Though that had been a wonderful experience, it was not authorization from the church but the calling of the Holy Spirit which was being confirmed to the church in Antioch as they had waited on Him for His choice, His guidance.

As for the two visits to Jerusalem, Professor Dunn suggests that the two visits to Jerusalem of Galatians 1:18 and 2:1 are correlated to Acts 9:26-30, and Acts 11:29-30, and so the letter to the Galatians can be dated before Paul was appointed to the Jerusalem Council of Acts 15, that is, before 49 A.D. (Dunn p 12). Paul was certain that his Damascus road epiphany, or Christophany, constituted his commission as an apostle, when he heard the voice of Jesus saying to him 'Saul, Saul, why do you persecute me?' (Acts 9:4). His whole life was changed by this encounter with Jesus. He says, 'God set me apart before I was born, and called me through His grace, and was pleased to reveal His Son to me and in me that I might preach Him among the Gentiles'. (Galatians 1:15).

God the Father had raised Jesus Christ from the dead, the resurrected One who had spoken to him on the Damascus road, and this same God had commissioned him to be an apostle to the Gentiles through the Lord Jesus Christ. (Galatians 1:1). No human agency had given him a licence to preach. He had been called by God, chosen to be an apostle of the Lord Jesus Christ, accountable only to Him.

This then was the right, the authority Paul had to write to the Galatian believers in this way. He was not self appointed, not an imposter. By challenging his apostleship, some of the Galatians were also challenging 'his' gospel, the gospel of justification by faith alone, with nothing added, nothing taken away; just the grace, the undeserved, unmerited favour of God to tormented sinners who wanted to approach a Holy God but who could not obey the law.

Galatians 1:2. 'And all the brethren who are with me'

Paul, an apostle .... and all the brethren who are with me. Grace to you and peace from God our Father and the Lord Jesus Christ.

In some of his letters, Paul mentions other 'brethren', brothers and sisters in Christ who are with him at the time of writing, and some who fulfill the role of an amanuensis or secretary. We have no means of identifying these brethren of verse 2, but we conclude that as this letter was written not long after Paul and Barnabas had completed their first missionary journey, both there and back through South Galatia; first in evangelism, then in establishing the congregations who had come to faith in Christ; and then by re-visiting them, 'returning to Lysta and Derbe, Iconium and Antioch in Pisidia, 'strengthening the souls of the disciples, exhorting them to continue in the faith and saying that through many tribulations we enter the kingdom of God', (Acts 14: 21,23), these brethren may have accompanied Paul and Barnabas from Antioch in Syria. Paul and Barnabas had suffered and endured many tribulations on that missionary journey.

They complete their journey where it had begun, in Syrian Antioch, going back to the north of Palestine, and as the letter to the Galatians was written not long afterwards, 'the brethren who are with me' may well have been brethren from the church in Syrian Antioch. This was before the Council in Jerusalem, Acts 15, where these same problems which were causing some anxiety in Antioch had apparently migrated to Jerusalem (Acts 15:1,2). By using the term, 'the brethren who are with me', Paul may have wished to convey that his views on justification by faith alone were held not only by him, but by colleagues and friends in Antioch too.

Galatians 1:3. Grace and peace

To the churches of Galatia, grace and peace to you from God the Father and the Lord Jesus Christ.

It is to this cluster of churches in Galatia; Lystra, Derbe, Iconium and Pisidian Antioch, that Paul writes, 'Grace to you and peace, from God the Father and the Lord Jesus Christ, who gave Himself for our sins to deliver us from this present evil age, according to the will of our God and Father, to whom be glory, *doxa*, (Gk), for ever and ever. Amen.

This is the gospel which Paul preaches. There can be absolutely no doubt that it is upon these great immutable truths that the Galatians, like the Thessalonians (1 Thessalonians 1:9,10) have turned from idols to serve the living and true God. Paul is stating very clearly the grounds upon which he is able to write to them, because he was the apostle through whom they had been able to come into the experience of saving faith. Through that faith, they had been welcomed as members of Christ's body, the church. The church in Galatia was one complete unity but was also local in expression and together the believers became the church in Galatia. So Paul could write to them collectively of the grace and peace which was theirs from God the Father and the Lord Jesus Christ.

It is to these deceived but beloved believers that Paul is writing 'grace and peace to you'. Though these were the normal words of greeting at the beginning of a letter, to both Paul and to those to whom he was writing they conveyed so much more.

Grace is God's attitude towards them. He wants them to understand that as sovereign Lord, He had provided for them a Saviour, one who had given Himself as a sacrifice for their sin, (Galatians 1:4), who would rescue them not only by the forgiveness of their past sins, but deliver them *from* the realm where sin is irresistible, the present evil age, *into* the realm where Christ is Lord. (Galatians 1:4; Titus 2:14). (Bruce p 75).

He has delivered them from this present evil age because that was His will for them, the grace of God through the Lord Jesus Christ who loved them and gave Himself for them. (Galatians 2:20,21). This was grace indeed, totally unmerited, totally undeserved and totally powerful and liberating, delivering them from all that would prevent them from coming to faith.

But how quickly were they attempting to turn from that grace to a 'different' gospel. (Galatians 1:6). This was astounding to Paul. They had received not only grace but peace and Paul was assuring them that God had not changed. His attitude towards them was still one of grace and peace. He wanted them to be not only in a state of grace but also in a state of peace, 'peace with God through our Lord Jesus Christ' (Romans 5:1); being content in their relationship with Him and with each other, content with the new life of faith ino which He had brought them, drawn by the gospel of the grace of God; safe from all outside forces which would seek to destroy or eliminate it.

There are elemental spirits, elemental powers of the universe (Galatians 4:3,9), but they are weak and beggarly, belonging to this present evil age, but to which the Galatians had once been enslaved. (Galatians 4:9). Did these believers want to exchange what they now had, to know God and to be known by Him, for a renewed bondage to beings that by nature are no gods? (Galatians 4:8). A bondage not to a godless world, but a world inhabited by so much that is antithetic to the gospel, and antipathetic to all that it stands for? So much worship is given to that which is not God.

Galatians 1:5. The doxology

To Him be glory for ever and ever. Amen

Paul cannot resist it. For all the grace and peace given to believers. For all the deliverance accomplished for them on the cross of Christ, where He poured out His life, Paul must give glory to God, the glory that will last for ever and ever. And he adds, 'Amen'. This is a doxology of thankfulness and worship to God which would encourage his readers to join him in the Amen, the endorsement of all that God had provided through His Son, according to the will of our God and Father.

To whom be glory, *doxa,* the unutterable effulgence of the Glory of God, denoting His divine presence, eternally. Amen. So let it come to pass, so may it be. So be it.

Jesus is Lord, our Lord Jesus Christ, (Galatians 1:3). In order to reverence the Name of God, YHWH, and not to take it in vain, (Exodus 20:7), the Hebrew scriptures used the word 'Adonai', my Lord, to substitute for the divine Name, which in the Greek or Septuagint version of the Hebrew scriptures becomes 'Kyrios', Lord. Kyrios in Greek usage could be a polite form of address to a stranger, 'sir', but in Christian circles began to stand for the full sense of 'lord', a confession of the deity of Christ as being *the* Lord, the Kyrios of the Old Testament, for He is YHWH, Adonai, Kyrios, my Lord and my God. (Cole p 70).

Jesus is Lord. There is no other Name under heaven given among men whereby we must be saved, and by which we may be translated out of this present evil age into the life of the age to come, everlasting, eternal life; from the power of Satan, God's adversary, to God. (Acts 4:12; 26:18) There is salvation in no one else.

This is the gospel preached by Paul. But he knows that among the Galatians 'there are some who trouble you and want to pervert the gospel of Christ'. (Galatians 1:7).

Galatians 1:6-9. The reason for the letter

> *I am astonished that you are so quickly deserting Him who called you in the grace of Christ and turning to a different gospel; not that there is another gospel, but there are some who trouble you and want to pervert the gospel of Christ. But if we, or an angel from heaven should preach to you a gospel contrary to that which we preached, let him be accursed. (Galatians 1:6-8).*

Paul had received news that a distressing situation had arisen in Galatia. There were believers who had come to faith in Christ, knowing that although they were Gentiles and not Jews, they were accepted by God into His family; and that they were part of the body of Christ.

But there were some among the believers who by race and nationality were Jews, who had come to faith in Christ but who were unwilling to leave behind their Jewish customs and traditions. They wanted to continue their observation of 'days, months, seasons and years (Galatians 4:10), the whole of the Jewish calendar. But additionally, they wanted their new Gentile brothers and sisters to do the same, to obey the law of Moses. Above all, they insisted that to truly become a Christian the Gentiles needed to be circumcised.

This had the potential to do two things. It could create a hierarchy of believers, those both Jews and Gentiles who were following Jewish customs, 'superior' believers; and those who were not. It also converted Christianity into a Jewish sect. Unless a believer was circumcised or born of a Jewish mother and whose father had been circumcised, he or she was not fully Christian.

This teaching was complete anathema to Paul. It was a complete reversal of the gospel. It was salvation by the works of the law, not by the hearing of faith. (Galatians 3:2,10). It was the perversion of the gospel into a different gospel, (Galatians 1:6), a gospel contrary to, and in fact in opposition to, the gospel preached to the Galatians by Paul and Barnabas. (Acts 13:2,5; 14:12).

Paul pleads with the Galatians not to be deceived 'by those who trouble you', (Galatians 1:7), 'those who would unsettle you', (Galatians 5:12), for to submit to their teaching is to turn away from the true gospel to a different gospel, and to desert Him who called them in the grace of Christ. They would fall from grace, they would be accursed, (Galatians 1:8), because they would be substituting the reality of gospel truth which was for all people, everywhere, and for all time, for a spurious gospel, limited in both objective and personnel and thereby making it of none effect, annulling it.

Paul writes that it is astonishing that this restrictive, shadow version of the gospel should have taken hold so quickly. It may be that the speed by which this alternative teaching has been accepted by the Galatian believers owed something to the disparagement of Paul's authority as an apostle, by 'the troublemakers', (Galatians 1:7), those agitators, who were encouraging the believers to doubt Paul's credentials. While he and Barnabas had been among them, they had listened eagerly to, and responded with alacrity to, all that had been spoken, but now Paul was a long way away, and how easy it is to forget, and even to embrace some new teaching.

When Paul first came among them, they welcomed him and though his condition was a trial to them, they did not scorn or despise him, but 'received him as an angel of light, of God'. (Galatians 4:14). Paul does not describe his symptoms, but does continue to write that if possible, they would have plucked out their own eyes and given them to him, (Galatians 4:15), which seems to be an obvious indication that there was something wrong with his eyes.

In such a short time, how had he become their enemy? (Galatians 4:16). Was it because the alternative teaching had become so persuasive, giving the Galatians the impression that they were indeed a very special elite people, although to Paul it had become obvious that they had become trapped, even if comfortably trapped, in their own little world.

Galatians 1:10-17. Paul's authority

> *Am I now seeking the favour of man or of God? Or am I trying to please men? If I were still pleasing men, I would not be a servant of Christ. For I would have you know, brethren, that the gospel which was preached by me is not man's gospel. For I did not receive it from man, nor was I taught it, but it came through a revelation of Jesus Christ. (Galatians 1:10-12).*

No wonder that Paul felt it necessary to emphasize his apostleship, his call to be an apostle to the Gentiles as well as to the Jews. He goes right back to the beginning of his fourteen (Galatians 2:1), or even seventeen (Galatians 1:18) years of experience, to establish his independence from any human agency. Though he had spent time in Jerusalem, he had received no authorization from anyone, not even from the apostles in Jerusalem who had been apostles before him, the leaders of the Jerusalem church.

Bruce quotes Calvin as noting that in attacking Paul, the troublemakers were attacking the truth of the gospel. (Bruce p 22). Paul is teaching that there is only one gospel. These trouble makers were claiming the possibility of other ways of living the life of faith, but this was heresy. Of course, Paul was defending himself and his apostolic authority against these false teachers, but this was not to establish his own teaching as orthodox while theirs was heretical, but because of the impossible situation into which his beloved Christian converts had been drawn. Before they came to Christ, had they been able to keep the law? The answer was 'no'. Then why, after they had been released from the bondage of the law by faith in Christ did they want to return to a yoke of slavery? (Galatians 5:1). Paul writes, 'My little children, with whom I am again in travail until Christ be formed in you', (Galatians 4:19), surely indicating how precious to him were the Galatian Christians.

Galatians 1:11-24. Paul's autobiography

> *For I would have you know brethren, that the gospel which was preached by me is not man's gospel. For I did not receive it from man, nor was I taught it, but it came through a revelation of Jesus Christ.. For you have heard of my former life in Judaism, how I persecuted the church of God violently and tried to destroy it. And I advanced in Judaism beyond many of my own age among my people, so extremely zealous was I for the traditions of my fathers. (Galatians 1:11-14).*

Paul feels it incumbent on him to expand his claim to the views he held, and he begins by reiterating his whole desire to please God. It appears from Galatians 1:10, that there had been a time when he had sought to please men. But he says, 'Now, am I seeking the favour of men or of God? Am I trying to please men? If I were still pleasing men I should not be a servant of Christ'. (Galatians 1:10).

Paul's former policy of trying to please men had been before he met the Lord Jesus Christ on the Damascus road. He had been diligent in seeking out those who called themselves 'the way', 'disciples of the Lord'; (Acts 9:1,2), that he might bring them, both men and women, bound to Jerusalem, there to be punished.

This ruthless behaviour was because he was convinced that this new phenomenon of people who were afterwards called Christians, (Acts 11:25), was undermining the Jewish faith to which he belonged, and which he felt so strongly to be a way of achieving righteousness before God. (Philippians 3:6). And this righteousness he felt he had achieved before any of his contemporaries, his own countrymen. (2 Corinthians 11:26). Paul says, 'I had advanced in Judaism beyond many of my own age among my people, so extremely zealous was I for the traditions of my fathers'. (Galatians 1:14).

This was when he was trying to please men rather than God, he says, although perhaps he was trying to do both at the same time, advancing in Judaism and also persecuting the church of God. He had discovered that to do this was nearly always a mistake, and almost always impossible. But this perceived inconsistency in his behaviour needed to be resolved and could only be resolved by a personal, life changing encounter with Jesus, the image of the invisible God whom he had been trying to serve. (Colossians 1:15).

Now writing to the Galatians, Paul is saying that these false brethren, brought in unawares, may have noted this inconsistency from his past, and were using it by applying it to Paul's present situation. Once inconsistent, always inconsistent, was the character flaw which they saw in Paul. (Galatians 2:4).

This was why Paul was determined that they should know that though he once sought to please men he did so no longer. All his thoughts, all his intentions were how to please God, but not in the old way of striving after perfect obedience to the law and thus achieving righteousness, but resting in the gift of righteousness won for him and all believers on the cross, the gift of being made righteous through faith in, and acceptance of, the righteousness of Christ.

The Galatian believers knew how much he had suffered while he was with them, (Acts 14:2,19; 13:50), a suffering which could have been avoided if he had not considered that his encounter with the risen Lord Jesus on the Damascus road had put him under a holy obligation to serve his Lord whatever the consequences.

He was called to serve Christ. The inconsistency, if there were now grounds for accepting that there was one, lay in the fact that Paul could not always serve Him and others at the same time. It was certain that though these people who wanted Gentiles to be circumcised in order to become fully Christian, had originally come to Christ in faith, Paul could not accept their false teaching when he saw what effect it had on his beloved believers.

Sometimes there was bound to be conflict and this applied both to those to whom he was bringing the gospel, some of whom rejected him; and also to the Christian leaders in Jerusalem with whom he wanted to retain fellowship while protecting his own independence of ministry, for he genuinely believed that the gospel which he preached came by revelation. Paul says of this personal revelation 'When He who had set me apart before I was born, and who had called me through his grace, was pleased to reveal His Son in me'. (Galatians 1:15).

It was not Paul's intention to please men, any men, by diluting the gospel or adding anything to the truth revealed in Jesus. (Ephesians 4:21). Inconsistency was the province of those who were exchanging the truth of God for a lie. (Romans 1:25). Men-pleasing? Inconsistency? No. Adaptability to situations? Yes; for example, Paul's taking of Timothy to be circumcised. (Acts 16:4).

But Paul describes himself as a slave of Jesus Christ, (Galatians 1:10; Philippians 1:1; Romans 1:1; Titus 1:1), placing himself unreservedly in the will of his Lord, for a slave is one who has no will of his own. He is only there to do his master's bidding, to do his master's will. And because of his status as a servant, a slave of Christ, he becomes also a slave of the church, 'with ourselves as your servants, slaves, for Jesus' sake' (2 Corinthians 4:5); his whole life dedicated to their service for that was the will of God concerning him. (1 Thessalonians 5:18).

Slaves cannot please another master, only the one who owns them. Paul was a servant, a slave of Jesus Christ. He was the one whom Paul sought to please. (Galatians 1:10).

Angels from heaven had throughout the scriptures approached human beings with truth. Paul says that God had not chosen to send an angel to the Galatians but a man like themselves. (Galatians 1:8). But even if He had sent them an angel, the message would have been the same that Paul preached to them; repentance towards God and faith towards our Lord Jesus Christ, for that was the gospel and that was sufficient.

The gospel preached by these false teachers was a false gospel, a perverted gospel. They were teaching that the gospel of Christ was not enough. It was the gospel *and*.... They had turned away from the gospel which was sufficient of itself to bring them into a right relationship with God through the Lord Jesus Christ, replacing it with the intention of having what seemed to them to be a fuller gospel, adding to it all that they had left behind on becoming Christians. They were impugning the word of God. They were saying that the gospel, the good news that the Lord Jesus had hung on the cross, becoming the bearer away of the sins of the world, including their sin, and had been raised from the dead to the glory of the Father, was not enough. They were saying, in effect, that the death of Christ on the cross was not enough to bring them into a relationship with God. Something more was needed. It was as though the Son of God had not done enough for their salvation.

This was perversion indeed. This was not the gospel which Paul preached. Paul's testimony to his estranged brethren was emphatic. He says, 'the gospel which was preached by me is not man's gospel, which your different gospel so patently is, because I did not receive it from men, nor was I taught it, but it came through a revelation of Jesus Christ'. (Galatians 1:11,12). He writes later in 2 Corinthians 3:14-16 that like many who had based their lives on the teaching of Moses, there had been a veil upon his mind. But when he turned to the Lord, the veil was taken away by the Spirit of the Lord. This was, and is, revelation, God's unveiling of truth to him; above all, revealing Christ to him.

But God had not only revealed His Son *to* him, but *in* him. The revelation of who Jesus was, and the indwelling of Jesus within his spirit had become part of him, informing his every action, every desire and every rational thought. He had been gifted by the Holy Spirit to come to faith, for faith is the gift of God. (Ephesians 2:8). This is the *received* gospel. And he was gifted by the Holy Spirit to come to understanding also, the *revealed* gospel, an understanding of the tremendous, wonderful truth which he had been able to share with these precious believers.

The gospel has been summarized in the formulaic phrase, Christ has died; Christ is risen; Christ will come again'; or in Paul's summary, Christ died for our sins in accordance with the scriptures, that He was buried, that He was raised on the third day in accordance with the scriptures. (1 Corinthians 15:3,4).

This was enough. Nothing else was necessary for faith, but to lay hold of this tremendous truth, that Christ loved me, and that He gave Himself for me. (Galatians 2:20). Everything flows from that. Paul had not received this gospel from man nor was he taught it by men, but it came through a revelation of Jesus Christ. (Galatians 1:12). This was the gospel of God concerning His Son, (Romans 1:1-3), imparted to him by no earthly authority or human agency, nor something he had reasoned by logical deduction, but revealed to him by the Lord Jesus, the risen Christ.

Kung writes that, to Paul, before his encounter with Jesus Christ, as to every other Jew, a crucified Messiah was an insult to the national political prophecies of the Hebrew Bible, and to their hopes that one day a Messiah figure would arise in their midst. Kung adds, such a concept, of a crucified Messiah, was absurd to them. They believed that their Messiah would be a man uniquely favoured by God (Isaiah 11:2), whereas a hanged man, according to Deuteronomy 21:23, was accursed by God.

Thus, to the Jews, the crucifixion of Christ made the idea of Jesus crucified as the Messiah completely illogical and in fact blasphemy, if not complete deception and misunderstanding, misinterpretation of the scriptures. (Kung p 39). This was what had given Saul/Paul the impetus, the motivation of giving himself wholeheartedly to the destruction of what he regarded as palpable lies, as he went about persecuting the church of God and violently attempting to destroy it. (Galatians 1:13).

This is why Paul later writes of the cross as a stumbling block, a scandal to Jews, what he later calls the offence of the cross. (1 Corinthians 1:23; Galatians 3:1; 5:11). God demonstrated His power and wisdom by allowing His Son to hang upon a cross. Christ had been publicly portrayed as crucified (Galatians 3:1), and this had been a stumbling block to many. (Galatians 5:11). But without it, there was no hope of eternal life for ransomed sinners. God had chosen that this was the pathway to Him, faith in a crucified God. Yet for those false brethren, those troublemakers, it was not enough. Their hope of salvation was still based on the perceived importance of circumcision and obedience to the law of Moses.

And it was because Paul did not preach circumcision that he was still being persecuted. (Galatians 5:11).

Galatians 1:13-17. Paul's conversion and confession

For you have heard of my former life in Judaism, how I persecuted the church of God violently and tried to destroy it. And I advanced in Judaism beyond many of my own age among my people, so extremely zealous was I for the traditions of my fathers. But when He who had set me apart before I was born and had called me by His grace was pleased to reveal His Son in me, in order that I might preach Him among the Gentiles, I did not confer with flesh and blood nor did I go up to Jerusalem to those who were apostles before me, but I went away into Arabia and again I returned to Damascus.

The Galatian believers knew of Paul's former life in Judaism, how he persecuted the church violently and tried to destroy it.

Paul had advanced in Judaism beyond many of his contemporaries, and was zealous for the traditions of his fathers. At that time, in his view, the followers of Jesus who were witnessing to the life and saving death and resurrection of Jesus were being blasphemous. Had God not revealed His Son to me and in me on the Damascus road, says Paul, I would have continued to regard the witness of those early disciples as blasphemous.

But by the grace of God to him, as one born out of due time, Christ appeared to him, and His grace towards him was not in vain. (1 Corinthians 15:8,10). From Paul's personal encounter with Jesus, whom Paul had persecuted when he had persecuted those who were followers of Jesus, (Acts 9:5), emerged a personal relationship with Him which became the absolutely dominating feature of his life. This wonderful encounter was the imperative to preach Jesus among the Gentiles, and kings, and the sons of Israel. (Acts 9:16). Paul wanted everyone to engage with Jesus and to receive new life in Him, just as he had.

Galatians 1:16,17. Time in Arabia

> Paul writes, *in order that I might preach Him among the Gentiles, I did not confer with flesh and blood, nor did I go up to Jerusalem to those who were apostles before me, but I went away into Arabia and again I returned to Damascus.*

The Galatian believers knew about Paul's former persecution of the church of God, (Galatians 1:16,17), but were perhaps unaware that Paul had not then gone up to Jerusalem to see the apostles, but had gone right away into Arabia, and then returned to Damascus.

His persecution of Christians should have disqualified him from becoming an apostle but he had been commissioned by God to preach to the Gentiles. He was 'sent' by God. That was what made him an apostle and even though there were others who had been apostles before him, he decided not to go immediately to Jerusalem to visit the apostles, even though he had made a short trip there after his vision on the Damascus road, when he had attempted to join the disciples in Jerusalem. (Acts 9:26). But he needed to spend some time alone in Arabia.

The whole essence of his call to apostleship through the appearance of the Lord Jesus Christ to him encouraged him to believe that some time spent alone with his Lord would help to equip him for the task which lay ahead, the promulgation of this outstanding experience for others; for though not all see a light from heaven and hear the voice of Jesus speaking to them, their experience of salvation, conversion, is just as valid, just as real, just as life-transforming.

Though Paul recognized that the twelve apostles in Jerusalem were regarded as leaders of the church in Jerusalem and that the time would come when there would be the necessity of commending his ministry to them and of maintaining good fellowship, Paul's immediate and urgent need was to spend intimate time with Jesus. This was the important next step. Paul went away into Arabia, an area south of Damascus and stretching away into the kingdom of Nabatea with its capital, Petra, whose king at that time was Aretas IV. (9 B.C-40 A.D). Though Paul's objective was for quiet communion with God in the wilderness, there had been an occasion when yielding to his ever-present imperative to preach the gospel, Paul had returned quietly to Damascus. But he had been arrested in Damascus at the instigation of the Jews, and only saved from Aretas by being let down in a basket over the wall; and thus saved by the disciples from being killed by the Jews, (Acts 9:23-28; 2 Corinthians 11:32); an experience which evidently made a deep impression on him.

How long Paul remained in Arabia we have no information, but he did return to Damascus and remained there for three years. (Galatians 1:18). Damascus was close to the territory surrounding Nabatea and there was a considerable Jewish community there. (Josephus; Bruce p 96).

From the disciples in Damascus, Paul derived much fellowship, (Acts 9:25), but it was not from them that Paul derived his gospel. It was not from man, however precious the fellowship may have been, but it came to him by revelation. God gave it. Paul received it. And it was the revelation of Jesus Christ. (Galatians 1:12). Jesus was not only the revealer, but the One revealed, the totality of whose life, death and resurrection were totally sufficient for the drawing of men and women into fellowship with Him.

Galatians 1:18-24. Paul in Jerusalem

> *Then after three years, I went up to Jerusalem to visit Cephas and remained with him fifteen days. But I saw none of the other apostles except James the Lord's brother. (In what I am writing to you, before God, I do not lie). Then I went into the regions of Syria and Cilicia. And I was still not known to the churches of Christ in Judea. (Galatians 1:18-22).*

Paul's three years in Damascus had come to an end. He was now ready to go up to Jerusalem. Paul had of course lived in Jerusalem as a student at the feet of Gamaliel, (Acts 22:3), but this visit to Jerusalem was different. He was privileged to spend fifteen days with 'Cephas', Peter's Semitic name, perhaps denoting the enormous respect for, and friendship, that Paul had with Cephas. At that time, Paul did not see any of the other apostles, except James the Lord's brother, who though not one of the twelve apostles, had become one of the leaders, perhaps the preeminent leader of the Jerusalem church. From John 7:5, we understand that the brothers of Jesus did not believe in Him during His earthly ministry, but that James was given a post resurrection appearance of the Lord, (1 Corinthians 15:7), who then appeared to all the apostles. Perhaps this was what gave James a distinctive place of leadership in the church.

But it was important to Paul to write to the Galatians that on this occasion of the visit to Cephas, he saw only Cephas and James. He says, in what I am writing to you, before God, I do not lie! Paul is comparing the gospel, that which has been revealed to him, with the traditions of the fathers, the traditions which these troublemakers want to impose on the church. (Galatians 1:14).

What was behind this emphatic declaration? Was it because the Galatian believers had not yet understood the seriousness of their situation; the significance of accepting a gospel contrary to that preached by Paul? (Galatians 1:9). Paul had already said 'as we have said before, so now I say again. If anyone is preaching to you a gospel contrary to that which you received, let him be anathema, let him be accursed'. (Galatians 1:9).

Paul is not cursing them, uttering imprecations against them. They are calling down a curse upon themselves, because they are not acknowledging Jesus as Lord; (1 Corinthians 12:3); they are speaking against the Holy Spirit, the One who glorifies Jesus. (John 16:14). Paul says, 'I want you to know brethren, I want you to understand; it is so important that you realize that the gospel which I preached was not man's gospel, as this 'different' gospel so obviously is, but it came to me by revelation'. (Galatians 1:12). His fellowship with Cephas and James was precious, but added nothing to the revelation he had received.

Is Paul saying that traditions are worthless? That only that which comes by revelation has any value, any merit? Paul had made a conscious decision to know nothing among them save Jesus Christ and Him crucified, just as he had when with the Corinthians. (1 Corinthians 2:2). And Paul adds to the Corinthians, 'I was with you in weakness and fear and much trembling, and my speech and message were not in plausible words of wisdom, but in demonstration of the Spirit and of power, that your faith might not rest in the wisdom of men but of God'. (1 Corinthians 2:4,5).

This was true both of his preaching to the Corinthians and of his ministry among the Galatians, for it was because of a bodily ailment that he preached to the Galatians at first. (Galatians 4:13). Even though Paul's whole testimony was based on 'Christ crucified', according to 1 Corinthians 2:2, he does not condemn all tradition, but only that which sets itself up against God, which is in conflict with the word of God.

Delivering to the Corinthian believers what he had himself received from God, in the example of the importance of celebrating their participation in the body and blood of the Lord at His table, had become tradition in the church, (1 Corinthians 11:23), as had also the tradition of setting aside a contribution for the saints on the first day of the week when it had become a tradition to meet together. (1 Corinthians 16:1,2). There are traditions which he advises the Thessalonian believers to hold onto as they had been taught by Paul, either by word of mouth or by letter. (2 Thessalonians 2:15). Paul is emphasising to the Thessalonians that all practices handed down to the church which become traditions must be in harmony with received revelation. 1 Corinthians 11:23 is the yardstick, the standard by which everything that Paul preaches must be judged. 'I passed on to you what I also received from the Lord'.

He observed that the tradition of head covering for women could be contentious, and he freely admits that on the matter of head covering he received no instruction from the Lord. (1 Corinthians 11:16). Paul does not insist upon head covering for women in the church, neither do the churches of God. *The importance of the concept of tradition being part of the revelation of what Christ is wanting His church to observe is what gives it its value.*

Paul had shown, just as Jesus had shown when confronting the Pharisees, that the traditions of the elders could separate men and women from God, (Matthew 15:3). At the time of Jesus, there were ways of observing these traditions which were available only to 'special' people, the elders. Jesus wants nothing to be allowed to come between the person who is seeking forgiveness, redemption, and a merciful God. He says to the elders, because of your traditions you have made void the word of God, you have emptied it of its meaning. (Matthew 15:6). What a terrible indictment this was of the religion practised by these Pharisees and scribes, those religious leaders who later came down from Jerusalem to entrap Him in His talk. (Matthew 22:15).

What Paul, following in his Master's footsteps, is writing against, fulminating against, is a new tradition which puts an *obstacle* in the way of those who want to enter into new life in Christ. This tradition had been brought in by 'troublemakers', agitators who considered that the gospel needed something extra to guarantee its acceptance. This was not the gospel. This was a distorted version of the gospel. It was not the gospel which was the power of God for salvation. (Romans 1:16).

There was an early tradition going back to Abraham and his walk with God, the tradition of justification by faith alone. (Genesis 15:6). This could be described as the true gospel. God preached this gospel beforehand to Abraham. (Galatians 3:8). This was the gospel revealed to Paul as it had been revealed to Abraham, that righteousness does not depend on 'works of the law', obedience to the law, for by the works of the law shall no man living be justified, be made right with God. (Galatians 2:16). The righteousness which is from God is by faith. Abraham was fully convinced that what God had promised He was able also to perform and this faith was reckoned to him as righteousness. (Romans 4:21,22). Righteousness is the gift of the grace of God and faith is the means by which men and women receive the gift; not of works, lest any man should boast. (Ephesians 2:9). This is the gospel.

Galatians 1:21-24. Paul in Syria and Cilicia

> Paul continues his testimony. He says, *'Then I went into the regions of Syria and Cilicia. And I was still not known by sight to the churches of Christ in Judea, they only heard it said that he who once persecuted us is now preaching the faith he once tried to destroy. And they glorified God in me.*

God, in His wisdom had allowed the Messianic age to begin, through the Messiah, through His Son, the Lord Jesus Christ, the incarnate Word of God. This was the conclusion which had taken hold of Paul. This was his conviction.

Paul was the privileged messenger of this wonderful truth. And after the time spent in Jerusalem with Cephas and James, Paul went into the regions of Syria and Cilicia with this life-transforming message. He had already preached to the Gentiles in Damascus. Now he was going to his own country, the place of his birth and early childhood.

He was from Tarsus in Cilicia, 'a citizen of no mean city'. (Acts 21:39; 22:3). After his brief visit to Jerusalem and a time of fellowship with Peter and James, Paul was now at liberty to go to Syria and Cilicia. He had shared with his brothers in Christ what had been revealed to him, and also what had been troubling him, and there was complete agreement between them at this time. It was only later that Peter began to have doubts around table fellowship, and he had a momentary stumble together with Barnabas about eating with Gentiles, but James had remained steady over the problem of circumcision and the law, which had become problematic for the churches in Galatia, although there was some problem for James also over table fellowship. (Galatians 2:12).

The two weeks in Jerusalem with Peter and James had been well spent, and Paul was now free to take the gospel to Syria and Cilicia.

At that time, Syria and Cilicia were a single Roman province and were administered by a Roman legate in Syrian Antioch. (Bruce p 103). Paul's brief statement of his visit to Syria and Cilicia agrees with the account in Acts 9:30 where it is recorded that Paul's Jerusalem friends took him down to the port of Caesarea and put him on a ship for Tarsus in Cilicia, from where he was later recruited by Barnabas in Acts 11:25 to teach in Antioch and to join in his apostolic work there, teaching a large company of people, 'and in Antioch the disciples were for the first time called Christians'. (Acts 11:26).

But Paul is meticulous about his Christian journey. He had met Barnabas before in Jerusalem after his encounter with the risen Christ on the Damascus road. (Acts 9:27). This was of course before his meeting again with him in Tarsus and his subsequent move to Antioch. Paul had spent some time in Tarsus which had become for him the headquarters of his fourteen years of ministry in Syria and Cilicia; fourteen years between the two Jerusalem visits of Galatians 1:18 and Glatians 2:1-10. The ministry in Tarsus was apparently very fruitful, as news of what was happening in Syria and Cilicia had reached both Antioch in Syria and also the churches in Judea, who heard it said that 'he who once persecuted the church is now preaching the faith which he once tried to destroy. And they glorified God in me. (Galatians 1:22-24).

Paul is quite deliberately maintaining that not only had he not been in contact with the Judean churches, he was not even known by sight to them. They had only heard about his preaching. (Galatians 1:22). But also that he had had no contact with the 'mother' church in Judea, that is, the church in Jerusalem, and describes these other churches rather loosely (though not in any way disparagingly), as 'the churches of Christ in Judea'. This was perhaps an indication that in Judea at least, the pernicious doctrine which he was seeking to eradicate in Galatia had not at this time infected Judea, although it is possible to infer from Acts 15:1 that it could be only a matter of time before this false perverted gospel could spread to other significant locations.

Paul is once again setting these two conflicting ideas of what it means to be a follower of Jesus, against each other, so concerned is he for the true, unadulterated gospel to be acknowledged, 'the faith which he had tried to destroy', (Galatians 1:23) the same faith, the same gospel.

Barclay, (p 14), comments on Paul's courage to go to Damascus where everyone knew of his former way of life and the persecution of believers, (Galatians 1:18), and then to Jerusalem where his former Jewish friends would regard it as harbouring a fanatic in their midst, or a traitor to their cause because he now refused to persecute those whom he had once despised; (Galatians 1:18); and then to Syria and Cilicia where he had grown up as a boy and as a youth and to whom his former childhood friends could have been unsympathetic, this person who had changed so much.

But Paul was quite prepared to be a fool for Christ's sake, (I Corinthians 4:10), says Barclay, (p 15), and to preach the gospel where it was hardest. For fourteen years he had laboured in the regions of Syria and Cilicia and was still unknown to the churches in Judea.

He was not seeking for any kind of worldly advancement, any kind of acknowledgement of the way God was blessing his ministry, of the many who were coming to faith in Christ. All that happened was that rumours would circulate. As one person heard the news about what was happening in Syria and Cilicia, he would pass it onto his friend. Nevertheless the glory went to God, 'they only heard it said that he who once persecuted the church is now preaching the faith which he tried to destroy. And they glorified God in me'. (Galatians 1:24).

If Paul was looking for any reward at all, which seems unlikely, the glory which went to God was reward enough.

The 'churches of Christ in Judea' may refer to those groups of believers who were scattered abroad after the persecution following the death of Stephen, (Acts 18:1), and evidently not churches founded by Paul. They were scattered throughout the region of Judea and Samaria. Bruce explains that at the time of Paul's letter to the Galatians, the Roman province of Judea also included Galilee and Samaria, (Bruce p 103), so that when Paul speaks of 'the church of God' in Galatians 1:13, he means in the first instance the believers in Jerusalem, but also, that as a result of persecution, the 'church in Jerusalem' had become 'the church in Judea' as its members scattered throughout Palestine, taking the gospel with them.

Paul may have been known by hearsay to the church in Jerusalem, but his point here is that he was not especially known to the Jerusalem church. But neither was he known to the Judean churches throughout the region of Palestine. *Paul is not elevating the Jerusalem church above the churches in Judea.* He is not giving to the church in Jerusalem any special priority. He recognizes that Jerusalem is not the only place of the Holy Spirit's activity but that throughout Judea believers are witnessing to the power of God in salvation, sharing a corporate life of faith and fellowship, and rejoicing in a personal relationship with the Lord Jesus Christ.

They may or may not have heard of Paul and his evangelical ministry in Syria and Cilicia, but he was undoubtedly unknown by sight to them. Even so, when they heard what he was doing, especially since he had formerly persecuted them, and there were potentially many with personal, individual memories of that persecution, they 'glorified God in me'. (Galatians 1:4). Every time they heard something more of what God was doing through their former persecutor, they gave thanks and praise to God.

It was part of Paul's defence of his apostleship among the Galatian believers, that the faith which he proclaimed was the same faith by which the Judean believers lived, worked, prayed and thanked God. This had been an encouragement to him during his fourteen years in Syria and Cilicia, and confirmation that he did not need authorization from the apostles in Jerusalem.

Galatians Chapter 2

Galatians 2:1-10. Paul's autobiography continues

A second visit to Jerusalem after his conversion.

Then after fourteen years, I went up again to Jerusalem with Barnabas, taking Titus along with me. I went up by revelation, and I laid before them, but privately, before those who were of repute, the gospel which I preach among the Gentiles, lest somehow I should be running or had run, in vain. (Galatians 2:1-3).

Fourteen years later, Paul had gone up to Jerusalem with Barnabas with whom he had had a precious time of ministry in Antioch. They had gone up to Jerusalem from Antioch in Syria, where they had carried on a ministry of teaching concentrated in Antioch for the last year. (Acts 11:26; 14:26). Paul says, 'I went up to Jerusalem again, together with Barnabas, taking Titus along with me'. So this is Paul's second visit to the Jerusalem church after his conversion, though he had known Jerusalem before in his pre-conversion days. On this occasion he was accompanied by Barnabas and Titus.

On his first visit, he had met only Peter and James the Lord's brother. Now he was about to meet 'those who were of repute' in the church, (Galatians 2;2), 'pillars in the church', (Galatians 2:9), James and Cephas/Peter and John. (Galatians 2:9).

Barnabas had been Paul's colleague, his co-worker in Syrian Antioch. He was a Levite, a man from a priestly family in Cyprus whose name was Joseph, but who was given the surname or soubriquet of Barnabas, son of consolation, son of encouragement; an indication of the kind of man he was. He was an early disciple in the Jerusalem church. (Acts 4:36).

After Paul's conversion, and his encounter with the resurrected Jesus on the Damascus road, Paul had remained for some time with the disciples at Damascus, but he aroused opposition among the Jews through preaching that 'Jesus is the Son of God' in their synagogues, and the Jews plotted to kill him. (Acts 9:23). This was the point at which Paul was let down over the wall in Damascus, in a basket by night, and escaped to Jerusalem. (Acts 9:25).

Paul's troubles were by no means over. When he came to Jerusalem, the disciples in Jerusalem were afraid of him because he had once persecuted the church, but Barnabas took him and brought him to the apostles, declaring how on the road, Paul had seen the Lord who spoke to him, and at Damascus he had preached boldly in the Name of Jesus. (Acts 9:26-29). Here again, in Jerusalem, the Hellenists, that is, Greek-speaking Jews, sought to kill him, and when the brethren knew of it, they brought him down to Caesarea and sent him off to Tarsus. (Acts 9:29). And no doubt Barnabas was of their number in their effort to protect Paul.

It was Barnabas who had first introduced Paul to the Apostles (Acts 9:27) and Barnabas who had been sent by the church in Jerusalem to Antioch who when he saw the grace of God among them was glad and exhorted them to be faithful to the Lord with steadfast purpose. 'For he was a good man, full of the Holy Spirit and of faith; and a large company was added to the Lord'. And it was Barnabas who went to Tarsus to look for Paul. (Acts 11:22-25).

The church in Syrian Antioch came into being as a result of the persecution of believers which arose after the death of Stephen, (Acts 11:19) and it had come to the attention of the church in Jerusalem that some of these believers, on coming to Antioch, spoke to the Greeks also, proclaiming the Lord Jesus. (Acts 11:20). 'And the hand of the Lord was with them, and a great number of those who believed turned to the Lord'. (Acts 11:21).

Paul, working together with Barnabas in Antioch saw for himself how Gentile and Jewish Christans lived together and worshipped together, and how no distinction was made between them on the grounds of their ethnicity. All were one in Christ. What drew them together was their faith in Him and their love for Him and for each other.

So it was from this ministry throughout Syria and Cilicia, that Paul went up to Jerusalem with Barnabas, taking Titus with them. (Galatians 2:1).

Titus was a Gentile Christian, one of the Greeks in Antioch who had heard the preaching of the word by the formerly persecuted believers in Jerusalem. He had believed and turned to the Lord. This was a precious example to Paul of what it meant to be a follower of the Lord Jesus Christ with no Jewish strings attached. (Galatians 2:3).

Paul went up to Jerusalem by revelation. This was a course of action which the Lord had revealed to him. He had not been invited by the Jerusalem church but knew from God that a serious discussion was necessary concerning the status of Gentiles within the wider church. He took Barnabas and Titus with him; Barnabas as a man full of the Holy Spirit and of faith, (Acts 11:24), and Titus as an uncircumcised Gentile believer.

Barnabas was already a seasoned and stalwart colleague, but Paul must have seen something in the young man Titus. Paul later writes of him in the second Corinthian letter as 'my brother Titus', whom he had hoped to find when he went to Troas but who had eventually joined him in Macedonia, northern Greece, and was a great comfort to Paul, and also to the church. (2 Corinthians 7:6,13).

Titus was also a practical man, concerned about the contribution made by the believers of Macedonia for those suffering from the famine in Jerusalem. Titus had already made a beginning for the relief of the saints and wanted to complete 'the 'gracious work of liberality'; for the Macedonian believers had given to the collection not only according to their means, but beyond their means, of their own free will, (2 Corinthians 8:1-6), and Paul was sending Titus to them, 'our brother, whom we have often tested and found earnest in many matters'; Paul's 'partner and fellow worker in your service'. (2 Corinthians 8:22,23).

This however was later. God had now shown Paul that he should go up to Jerusalem and take Barnabas and Titus with him, with the intention of communicating 'privately before those who were of repute' in Jerusalem, (Galatians 2:2), the gospel which he preached among the *Gentiles*, lest somehow he should be running, or had run in vain.

This appears to be an acknowledgement that Paul thought it was expedient to have the approval of the men of repute in Jerusalem. But it was not their authorization which he needed. That was a different issue altogether. He had already claimed that the only authorization he required came from God through revelation. He had not conferred with flesh and blood, with human beings concerning the gospel. (Galatians 1:6). It was not man's gospel, (Galatians 1:11) it came through a revelation of Jesus Christ. (Galatians 1:12). Jesus had revealed Himself to Paul. Jesus had authorized him to preach to the Gentiles *and* to the sons of Israel. (Acts 9:15).

What Paul wanted was that the leaders in Jerusalem should understand that the gospel which Paul preached among both Jews and Gentiles was the same gospel which they themselves preached. Paul was concerned that it should be, and in fact was, the same gospel. He could later write to the Corinthian church, 'whether it was I who preached (or Cephas or James), so we preached and so you believed'. (1 Corinthians 15:11). The saving, delivering power was in the gospel, in the message and not in the messenger.

Galatians 2:4,5. False brethren

> *But because of false brethren secretly brought in, who slipped in to spy out our freedom which we have in Christ Jesus that they might bring us into bondage – to them we did not yield submission, even for a moment that the truth of the gospel might be preserved for you.*

This was the message of Paul and the message of the leaders in Jerusalem was the same. It was no longer necessary to keep the Jewish law, or to be circumcised in order to be fully redeemed. It was only necessary to trust in the saving power of the sacrifice of Christ upon the cross. As proof that Paul and the leaders of the Jerusalem church were in total agreement over the issue, the Jewish Christian leaders of the church in Jerusalem had no desire to compel Titus to be circumcised even though he was a Greek, of Gentile origin. (Galatians 2:3).

But a problem arose, and it was an acute problem. Paul notices that 'false brethren were *secretly* brought in, who slipped in to spy out our freedom which we have in Christ Jesus, that they might bring us into bondage'. (Galatians 2:4).

This may have been why Paul wanted to consult with the Jerusalem leaders who were of repute, 'privately'. (Galatians 2:2). He needed to know exactly where those men of repute stood in relation to these false brethren. Paul had enjoyed the time he had previously spent with Peter and James, but at that time, these false brethren, troublemakers as Paul calls them in Galatians 1:7, had not made their appearance. Now, fourteen years later, the problem had become acute; its implications serious; the whole of the Christian message compromised.

It was not only that Paul was concerned about his own ministry, that perhaps his labour had been in vain. (Galatians 2:2; Phillipians 2:16). His concern was that the whole purpose of God in relation to the ultimate destiny of men and women and their present experience of knowing life to the full as they committed their lives to Christ, was in danger of being completely annulled, cancelled, made of none effect, because their faith would not be in Christ alone, the solid ground of their acceptance before God; they would be trusting in a counterfeit gospel, a false gospel. And they would be brought into bondage. (Galatians 2:4). This would be the result, perhaps unforeseen, perhaps unpremeditated or perhaps deliberate, of these false brethren 'brought in secretly to spy out our freedom which we have in Christ, that they might bring us into bondage'.

Paul declares, 'to whom we did not yield submission, even for a moment, that the truth of the gospel might be preserved for you', the Galatian believers, his brothers and sisters in the Lord. (Galatians 2:5).

Paul cannot understand how anyone would want to exchange this gospel of free grace for all, both Jews and Gentiles; the truth of 'his' gospel; for a mutilated gospel. He could not submit to a false teaching which denied to these Galatian Christians the whole integrity for which the gospel stood; for justification, that is, being made righteous before God by faith alone, and not by attempts to satisfy a Holy God by one's own efforts; and for receiving the Holy Spirit as a gift of God's grace, regardless of the ethnicity of the recipient. Paul will not accept, under any circumstances, the subversion of the gospel advocated by these false brethren, compelling Gentiles to live like Jews. (Galatians 2:14).

All that Paul describes of these false brethren is that 'they slipped in to spy out our freedom which we have in Christ Jesus'. He may have known them by name, but he does not identify them. This infiltration may have originated in Judea, the province in which Jerusalem was situated, for in Acts 14:26-5:1,2, there is a reference to men who came down *to* Antioch *from* Judea, teaching the brethren, 'unless you are circumcised, according to the custom of Moses, you cannot be saved'. (Acts 15:1).

And it was from Antioch that Paul and Barnabas were appointed by the church to go up to Jerusalem to the apostles and elders about this question (Acts 15:2).

But it appears that this present visit to Jerusalem described in Galatians 2 took place before the (third) visit to Jerusalem of Acts 15. We conclude that it was already becoming a problem, a potentially divisive problem in the church as a whole, a division between those who were prepared to live alongside and love one another whatever their background, and others who held fast to 'the traditions of the fathers'. (Galatians 1:14).

And this was a problem which was already becoming acute for the churches in Judea before Paul and Barnabas left Antioch. This visit may well have been a preliminary visit before the visit to Jerusalem which took place *before* the Council of Jerusalem in Acts 15, and the Apostolic Decree; especially as Paul describes this visit as taking place 'privately'. (Galatians 2;2). The Council of Jerusalem was very public and highly controversial.

These factors indicate that Paul, Barnabas and Titus had arranged this vital visit to Jerusalem as a warning to the church of what the consequences would be if this perverted gospel was allowed to take hold. Paul had related to the Galatians what had taken place on a previous visit so that they could avoid being deceived by what appears to have been an attempt by these troublemakers to undermine their status as *Gentile* Christians of Galatia and at the same time to undermine the status and experience of Paul and his companions as those set free from the Law, and rejoicing in the freedom which they had in Christ, because it was for freedom that Christ had set them free. (Galatians 5:1).

Traditionally, these false brethren have been known by interpreters, exegetes of Paul's letters as 'Judaizers', meaning those Jewish Christians who attempted to bring other believers within Judaism. But Professor Dunn explains that the word Judaizer is drawn directly from the Greek, and means to live just like a Jew, observing Jewish customs but *not* imposing Judaism on others. He continues, that this inaccurate meaning of Judaizer implies a strong evangelistic zeal to bring others into Judaism which is not borne out in contemporary literature, although, as we see for example in the story of Cornelius in Acts 10, God fearers and proselytes were always welcome in Jewish synagogues. The only full scale missionary movement of which we are aware is that of Jews who had believed in Jesus as the prophesied Messiah, and who wanted others to know Him too. (Dunn p 10).

Paul does not call them Judaizers, but he does call them false, perverters of the gospel, troublemakers, and describes fully in Galatians the trouble they have caused, and of what it consists. Though Paul is recounting to the Galatians an earlier visit to Jerusalem, he is now writing this letter to the Galatians warning them of the present peril and danger to them of the false teaching of these false teachers.

It has been noted that the letter to the Galatians was written while Paul was in Antioch of Syria after his first missionary journey with Barnabas, when he had travelled with Barnabas through Perga and Pamphylia to the other Antioch, Antioch in Pisidia, in the province of Galatia. (Acts 14:24-26), giving the impression that though these false brethren had continued their infiltration of the church in Syrian Antioch, the problem had become widespread and was now urgent and something that Paul had to deal with. These verses suggest that it was after the writing of this letter to the Galatians, while he was still in Antioch of Syria, that Paul and Barnabas were requested by the church to take the matter to the Jerusalem council of Acts 15.

So the chronology, attempting to harmonize the account in Acts with the Galatian letter would be:-

The commissioning of Paul and Barnabas by the Holy Spirit in the church in Antioch of Syria, followed by preaching to the Galatians and establishing a church in Galatia, in Pisidian Antioch, Iconium, Lystra and Derbe, (Acts 13:13-14-24). Then returning to Antioch in Syria to report back to the brethren there, writing to the Galatians about the need for vigilance because of the false brethren, and subsequently going up to Jerusalem on a second visit. Then the return to Antioch in Syria and being appointed by the church there to go up to Jerusalem (the third visit), for discussion and resolution of the heretical problem caused by the false brethren.

This chronology does not accord with all biblical scholarship. Professor Bruce says that the majority view is that the infiltration of false brethren took place during the Jerusalem visit described by Paul in Galatians 2: 1-10, and that the infiltrators wormed their way into the discussion between Paul, Barnabas, Titus and the pillars of the church, James, Cephas and John, and demanded that Gentile converts, in particular Titus, should be circumcised. (Bruce p 115). But Bruce has an alternative view. He says, where else could false brethren have intruded but into the headquarters of the Gentile mission in Antioch?

The preceding view could be justified on the grounds that in both instances, the issue under discussion was circumcision, but it makes the non-circumcision of Titus a parenthesis, when it is obviously part of Paul's argument about the solidarity of the message as preached by both the Jerusalem church and his own ministry, though of course the issue of circumcision need not have been confined to one visit only.

Whichever alternative is preferred, the main point of the presence of Paul, Barnabas and Titus in Jerusalem at this time is concerned with this 'supplementary' gospel, the gospel with so-called added refinements, brought to Jerusalem by these infiltrators.

Paul needs to establish his credentials before these men of repute in Jerusalem, that he had not run, nor was running, in vain. (Galatians 2:2). Though these men were the leaders of the church in Jerusalem, they were not therefore to be especially regarded and listened to, for God shows no partiality, (Galatians 2:6). All are servants of His and unless commissioned by Him, have no authority at all.

Paul is not accusing them of having no validity in their teaching, or questioning their personal integrity. He is simply aware that by implying their spiritual authority to be above his own would lead to a jeopardizing of the integrity of all those who had come to Christ through his ministry and therefore to a diminution of their experience of the life giving experience of their salvation from sin, and the infilling of the Holy Spirit. (Galatians 3:3).

Cephas/Peter and John had been with Jesus throughout His earthly ministry. They had had the privilege of being with Him during those final days of His death, resurrection and ascension into heaven. They had heard His words of promise as He was parted from them and a cloud received Him from their sight. They had been among those who had received the Holy Spirit on the day of Pentecost.

Jesus had said to them, 'You shall receive power after that the Holy Spirit has come upon you and you will be witnesses to Me in Judea, and Samaria, and to the uttermost parts of the earth'. (Acts 1:8,9). They had been entrusted with the gospel to the Jews while Paul had been entrusted with the gospel to the Gentiles, though this was a generalization, for Peter and John, and also Paul, all had times when they were constrained by the Holy Spirit to preach to both Jews and Gentiles.

Because James and Peter and John, those pillars of the church, perceived the grace that was given to Paul and Barnabas, 'they gave to Paul and Barnabas the right hand of fellowship', that they should go to the Gentiles while Peter, James and John went to the circumcision, that is, to the Jews. (Galatians 2:9). Peter's mission to the Jews, and Paul's mission to the Gentiles were equally blessed by divine approval as signs and wonders accompanied their proclamation of the gospel. (Acts 5:12,15; 19:11-16). There were not two gospels but one.

But the agitators were attempting to introduce two gospels, a different gospel from that preached by both Peter and Paul. (Galatians 2:6). This different gospel was not a gospel *of circumcision*, but a gospel *for the circumcision*, that is, the Jews, those who had been accustomed from childhood to listening to the words of Moses which were read in every synagogue, every Sabbath. (Acts 15:21). But circumcision could not bring them freedom from doing the works of the law. For that they needed Jesus. They needed to know that in going to the cross for them, dying for them, Jesus had rendered their own efforts at achieving some merit with a Holy God null and void, empty of any value whatsoever in terms of righteousness before Him.

Jesus had done it all. He had taken away their sin, had allowed their efforts at holiness to be of no avail as they trusted in Him, for however hard they tried they could never reach the total spotlessness of the Lamb of God who takes away the sin of the world. From now on, as those who had come to faith in the finished work of the Lord Jesus all they had to do was to lean on Him for His mercy when they did fall; for His grace, for His love for them, knowing He had a purpose for their lives.

And there were some who would take all that away from them and cause them to revert to their former state. No wonder Paul was white hot with grief and indignation, and astonishment that these beloved Galatian Christians could ever contemplate turning to a 'different gospel', and representing the death of Jesus as being of none effect.

Galatians 2:10. Remembering the poor

James, Cephas and John, who were reputed to be pillars, gave to me and Barnabas the right hand of fellowship, so that we might go to the Gentiles, and they to the circumcised. They only asked us to remember the poor, the very thing I also was eager to do. (Galatians 2:9,10).

Peter, James and John had recognized 'the grace given to Paul' (Galatians 2:9) and his apostleship to the Gentiles. Paul was a pioneer apostle; they were commissioned differently by God, for it was important to have a 'mother' church in the early days of Christianity.

Paul's use of the term 'pillar' for the leaders of the Jerusalem church is repeated in John's apocalyptic writing, where he writes of the angel of the church in Philadelphia conveying the message that 'he who overcomes I will make a pillar in the temple of my God and I will write upon him the Name of my God'. (Revelation 3:12). A pillar in the sanctuary, the temple, was what the church in Jerusalem and its leaders had become, representing stability and security for the infant church.

The leaders of the church had not at this time received recognition as 'bishops' or 'overseers'. But, Paul says, they are pillars. They have their special place, their special function. It is given to them by God, just as He had given Paul's to him. They were two different spheres of ministry and these five men clasped each other's hands in fellowship, in recognition of it. The age of the law had become the age of the Spirit. (Galatians 3:13,14). There may be diversity among believers. There is also an essential unity. They are all one in Christ Jesus.

But this diversity extended not only to their backgrounds, their culture, the ministry which was given to them by the Lord, but also to their material needs. The elders in Jerusalem were only too well aware of those who were suffering from the famine, and may well have done all they could to alleviate it. But they needed help. Would Paul, Barnabas and Titus assist them to meet the needs of these struggling believers? And of course the answer was 'Yes'. 'The leaders of the church would have us remember the poor, which very thing I was eager to do', says Paul. (Galatians 2:10).

Paul had already been made aware by the prophecy of Agabus in Acts 11:27-30, that there would be a famine in the time of the emperor Claudius, causing the disciples in Antioch, each according to his ability, to send relief to the brethren in Judea. 'And they did so, sending it to the elders by the hands of Barnabas and Paul'. (Acts 11:30).

Cole explains that there were several causes for the chronic poverty of the church in Judea. Palestine at that time was overfilled and overpopulated, and chronic rebellions and disturbances had worsened the position already made grave by the generally barren nature of the soil after more than a millennium of deforestation. (Cole p 112). Cole compares the Palestine of that time with villages in Africa or India today. In addition, the land was perpetually crowded by pilgrims returning to their homeland for the Jewish festivals.

Paul had already made a collection for the saints in Jerusalem, and in a sense did not need to be reminded to 'remember the poor'. But it was always in Paul's heart to encourage believers to share whatever they had.

This is the second good thing to come out of this visit of Paul, Barnabas and Titus to Jerusalem; the first being the right hand of fellowship, and now a common consent to remember the poor, the very thing that Paul was eager to do. This is more than confirmed by Paul's later relief fund following his ministry in Macedonia. (1 Corinthians 16: 1-4; 2 Corinthians 8:1-9:15; Romans 15:25-28). Even in this early letter to the Galatians, Paul is encouraging the believers to bear one another's burdens, and so fulfil the law of Christ, (Galatians 6:2), a happy sharing of one another's burdens, and not only their material burdens, but in every way possible; not because they ought to, but because it was in their heart to do so, spontaneously, without compulsion, for God loves a cheerful giver. (2 Corinthians 9:5-7).

And Titus had a hand in this too, for he was not only a comfort to Paul and the church (2 Corinthians 7:6), but Paul had urged him that as he had made a beginning of supplying the needs of the believers in Jerusalem, so he would complete 'this gracious work', this work of grace. (2 Corinthians 8:6). This of course comes later. But on this visit to Jerusalem, Titus was just as eager as Paul to 'remember the poor', in response to the request from the elders of the church in Jerusalem and wherever the Lord's people had need.

Galatians 2:11-17. Conflict in Antioch over table fellowship

> *But when Cephas came to Antioch, I opposed him to his face because he stood condemned. For before certain men came from James he ate with the Gentiles, but when they came, he drew back and separated himself, fearing the circumcision party.*
>
> (Galatians 2:11,12).

Paul and Peter had already exchanged the right hand of fellowship, so why was it necessary for Paul to remember an occasion when Peter had come to Antioch, and he had questioned Peter about table fellowship?

Paul's remembrance of the occasion was acute. He remembered vividly that he had 'opposed Peter to his face because he stood condemned'. Before certain men came to Antioch from James, Peter had been happy to eat with the Gentile Christians, but when they came, bearing with them the authority which they believed was invested in James and the Jerusalem church, Peter drew back and separated himself, fearing the circumcision party, that is, Jews who had become Christians. (Galatians 2:11,12).

And not only Peter but the rest of the Jewish Christians also acted insincerely, so that even Barnabas was carried away by their insincerity. (Galatians 2:13). Paul's trusted friend and colleague Barnabas, 'son of consolation', could see this as only a temporary problem. While the party from Jerusalem were with them he would not grieve them. He would abstain from eating with the Gentiles, but once they had returned to Jerusalem, normal terms of fellowship could be resumed. (Cole p 117).

But there was a greater significance to this episode than either Peter or Barnabas realized. There was a breach opening up between Antioch and Jerusalem. The Jews from Jerusalem saw in Antioch a threat to Jewish distinctiveness, and to combat this, were attempting to maintain as far as possible a social life apart from Gentiles, even Gentile Christians, including a concern to maintain Israel's covenant obligations. (Dunn p 14, 78).

This had become a matter of tremendous concern to Paul, which was why it had to be addressed publicly, both 'to Peter's face', (Galatians 2:11), and 'before them all'. (Galatians 2:14). Paul's accusation of Peter was that he had not been straightforward about the truth of the gospel, the truth that *no one whether Jew or Gentile had any hope of being accepted by God*, of being able to stand before His judgement seat with any claim of being accepted by Him. *Only by wearing the robes of righteousness purchased for men and women on the cross had they any hope of acceptance.* On that day, God will not say, 'Did you eat with Gentiles?', but 'Did you reverence My Son? Love Him? Worship Him?'.

Paul's aim was not the public exposure of Peter but that the truth of the gospel might be preserved, *the precious unity of all believers whatever their ethnic origin.* This was of such great concern to Paul. He shares the same gospel as Peter. His gospel is not different from Peter's. They both rightly claim that their ministry comes from God. Did the believers at Antioch have a choice, either to believe Paul's gospel or Peter's? Could there have been the beginning of a faction in the church in Antioch? Some might argue, 'Let us go with Peter', while others thought, 'no, I think Paul's teaching is right'.

Galatians 2:15-21. Justification by faith alone

But when I saw that they were not straightforward about the truth of the gospel, I said to Cephas before them all, 'If you, though a Jew, live like a Gentile and not like a Jew, how can you compel the Gentiles to live like Jews? We ourselves who are Jews by birth and not Gentile sinners yet who know that a man is not justified by works of the law but through faith in Jesus Christ, even we have believed in Christ Jesus in order to be justified by faith in Christ and not by works of the law because by works of the law shall no one be justified (Galatians 2:14-16).

Paul's letter to the Galatians does not make explicit when this incident happened, but its importance cannot be denied. Circumcision of Gentile believers, reliance on obedience to the law, maintaining ancestral traditions such as the Jewish food laws, did it really matter if there were two Christian groups, living alongside each other with their own distinctive way of being Christian? Why had Paul reacted so violently to the behaviour of Peter and Barnabas?

There was no ambiguity about Paul's reaction. Even had there been in all other respects equality between the two groups of believers Paul would still have been concerned for the Gentile believers in Antioch who were not allowed to be in full fellowship with their Jewish brothers and sisters. This social separation implied that they were second class Christians, inferior because their Christianity was defective in some way.

Cole suggests (p 114) that this incident may have taken place when Peter left Jerusalem after his miraculous escape from prison, at the time of the death of John the brother of James under Herod's cruel regime. In Acts 12:17, we read that Peter departed from Jerusalem where he had been imprisoned and went to another place, unwilling to remain in Jerusalem where he could put other believers at risk. This place is identified by Cole in Acts 12:19 as Caesarea, a city not far from Antioch in Syria.

But we have no evidence for this or even how long he had stayed in Antioch if that was indeed the church to which he had gone. But we do know that Barnabas and Saul/Paul were in Antioch at that time, (Acts 13:1) and in Galatians, Paul has regretfully to announce that even Barnabas was carried away by their insincerity, the insincerity of those who came down from James in Jerusalem, and was carried away by their dissimulation, their deceitful manipulation of the gospel.

Apart from Peter's speech at the council of Jerusalem in 49 A.D., Acts 12:19 is the last reference we have to Peter in the Acts of the Apostles. Peter had become a man of peace. His life had been totally transformed by the death and resurrection of his Master whom he had learned to love during those three years of His ministry; and by the power of the Holy Spirit which had come upon him at Pentecost.

He had been given so much, and what he had been given he wanted to share with others, but that could involve compromise. Within that attempt at conciliation lay the seeds of trouble for the future. When 'certain men' came down from James, Peter and Barnabas drew back from eating with the Gentile Christians and separated themselves, 'fearing the circumcision party', those Jewish Christians who had refused to give up their allegiance to the law of Moses.

This may have indicated that Peter and Barnabas not only did not eat at the common table with Gentile Christians, but even more significantly that they did not share the Lord's table with them. If this was the case, then the situation was desperate. This group of extremists from Jerusalem were dividing the whole church in Antioch into two opposing groups, the circumcision party on the one hand and the inferior Gentile Christians on the other. This may well have occasioned Paul's outburst to the Corinthian believers, 'there is one Body, the body of Christ, and there is one Bread, and we who are many are one body because we all share in the one bread'. (I Corinthians 10:17).

Was Peter separating himself from the Gentile believers because he hoped in that way to maintain fellowship with what was represented by the men from James? So that the churches of Antioch and Jerusalem could still be on terms of fellowship with one another? Was it an attempt to accommodate both points of view? Peter was in an altogether invidious position, trying to maintain fellowship with both groups. But at what a cost. Cole describes it as 'peace at any price'. (Cole p 117).

But Paul was not prepared for peace on those terms. He opposed his beloved friend and brother 'to his face' because he stood condemned. (Galatians 2:11). He respected Peter and his ministry as an apostle before him. (Galatians 1:17). Peter was his brother in Christ. But there was too much at stake here. It was and had to be, full on, a public head on collision because of the truth of the gospel. There is neither Jew nor Greek, bond or free, for we are all one in Christ Jesus. (Galatians 3:28).

Galatians 2:14-17. All one in Christ

But when I saw that they were not transparent, not straightforward about the truth of the gospel, I said to Cephas before them all, 'If you, though a Jew live like a Gentile, and not like a Jew, how can you compel the Gentiles to live like Jews? (Galatians 2:14).

Peter is contradicting the principle so precious to Paul, that there is neither Jew nor Greek, slave or free, male or female, for we are all one in Christ Jesus. (Galatians 3:28). All are justified, made righteous, not by the outward sign of circumcision, or by keeping the law or by abstaining from eating with Gentiles even if they happen to be Christians. They are made righteous by faith alone, 'for he who who is made righteous by faith shall live' (Galatians 3:11). Paul is speaking of the just, the justified, those made righteous and who live by faith in Jesus; for no one is made righteous by the works of the law.

Paul is emphatically declaring to Peter what he already knows, that we ourselves who are Jews by birth and not Gentile sinners, (that is, people who were not chosen by God to be His people), *we ourselves know* that a man is not justified by the works of the law, but through faith in Christ; *even we* have believed in Christ Jesus in order that, so that, we will be justified by faith in Christ, and not by the law, for we know that by the works of the law can no one living be justified, (Galatians 2:15-16).

Paul, though born a Jew, had been living like a Gentile ever since encountering the risen Lord Jesus on the Damascus road, and becoming a follower of Him. But Peter had also been born a Jew and he too had been living like a Gentile ever since Jesus had interrupted his fishing expedition one morning and said to him, 'Follow Me'. So Paul says to Peter, 'how can you now compel Gentiles to live like Jews?' It did not work for you. How can you expect it to work for them?

Peter and Paul were agreed on one thing, and it was the most important thing of all. Through faith in Christ, through accepting the fact that we are all sinners before a righteous God, both Jews and Gentiles, and desperately in need of the provision of the forgiveness of our sins, which Christ won for us on the cross, we *all belong to Hm.*

All of us, both Jews and Gentiles come to Him by way of the cross. God makes no distinction between us. He imposes no conditions upon us. He gives to all of us the privilege of fellowship with Him. So what right do we have to withhold fellowship from those who are different from us, to impose conditions upon them which He does not impose?

Anything that divides us from one another; ethnicity, social status, religious convictions, circumcision, works of the law, with whom we share our food; all these and other hindrances to our fellowship with one another, have to go. We are all one in Christ Jesus. We are all part of the one body which is Christ; the diverse, and united family of God.

Later, in writing to the Roman believers, Paul says, 'Receive one another as Christ has received you'. (Romans 15:7). Peter may have been born a Jew, even as Paul had, but they were no longer bound by family or institutional ties. They had both been given new life in Christ, a new future, a new destiny, living daily in the light of the resurrection of Jesus Christ. It is true that believers do strive for peace with all, as Peter had done, but only because they know that striving for peace, they are also striving for holiness without which no one will see the Lord. (Hebrews 12:14).

Stott says, we need to hear again the heavenly voice which Peter heard on the roof of the house of Simon the tanner. 'Do not call anything unclean that God has made clean. What God has cleansed you must not call common'. (Acts 10:15). Although the vision Peter had received challenged the basic distinction between clean and unclean *foods*, the Spirit related this to the distinction between 'clean' and 'unclean' *people*. So Peter understood that 'God has shown me that I may not call any one impure or unclean'. (Acts 10:28. Stott p 187)

Galatians 2:15-21. Paul's final comment on Antioch

We ourselves, who are Jews by birth and not Gentile sinners yet who know that a man is not justified by works of the law but through faith in Christ, even we have believed in Christ Jesus, in order to be justified by faith in Christ and not by works of the law because by works of the law shall no one be justified. But if in our endeavour to be justified we ourselves are found to be sinners, is Christ then an agent of sin? Certainly not! But if I build up again those things which I tore down, I make myself a transgressor. (Galatians 2:15-18).

Though Paul is still remembering the incident in Antioch with Peter and Barnabas, as an example of how easily the truth of the gospel can become so brutally misconceived, leaving some believers on the periphery of fellowship; reducing them to the status of second class Christians; it appears that in his thought he has temporarily moved on from Antioch. And he has become very personal in his assessment of life in Christ, and in what he regards as the normal Christian life.

Though he had been gloriously justified by faith in Christ, this does not mean that he never sins. He has not reached sinless perfection. He is still in the process of sanctification, becoming separated unto God, the power of the cross dealing daily with anything that could militate against a pure and utter devotion to this one whom he has come to love; his Lord.

He has come under the healing, cleansing power of the cross of Jesus and yet he is found to be still one who is capable of sinning. Is Christ then an agent of sin? God forbid!, Certainly not! No, never! me genoito! (Gk) says Paul, (Galatians 2:17) as he recoils in absolute horror at the idea. How could Jesus promote wrongdoing? It is utterly inconsistent with all that he has come to know of the character of Jesus. It is blasphemy because it also implies that justification, coming to us through the cross of

Christ, is an abstract status, a legal fiction which does not result in a change in moral behaviour.

But justification, being made righteous through faith in Christ, is no legal fiction. It is a renewed state of being. In writing to the Corinthians, Paul says, 'If anyone is in Christ, he is a new creation. The old has passed away; the new has come'. (1 Corinthians 5:17). And to the Ephesians, 'You He made alive when you were dead through your trespasses and sins, in which you once walked'. (Ephesians 2:1). Newly alive; new life in Christ.

We can never come to a state of righteousness by obeying the works of the law; we must always be conscious that we stand before a Holy God. We have nothing to bring Him, no effort of ours will ever be enough to satisfy Him. But Jesus fully satisfied His Father. He was the spotless Lamb of God. And because He was spotless, He could take away the sin of the world. (John 1:29). All who trust in the death that He died to take away sin, and the glorious affirmation by God that through His death and resurrection He has put away sin by the sacrifice of Himself (Hebrews 9:26), are justified. It is the only way for anyone to claim to be righteous. But he who is made righteous by faith shall live. (Romans 1:17).

Justification is a positive act on the part of God to make those righteous who otherwise would have no hope of coming before a Holy God. And strange as it may seem, it is because God wanted a chosen race, a royal priesthood, a holy nation, a people for His own possession. (1 Peter 2:9). He wanted to bring many sons to glory, (Hebrews 2:10). He wanted a Bride for His Son, (Ephesians 5:35-32; Revelation 21:2), 'without spot or wrinkle or any such thing, that she should be holy and without blemish before Him'. (Ephesians 5:27).

And all this and more, Christ accomplished on the cross, so that being justified by faith, men and women could have peace with God through our Lord Jesus Christ. (Romans 5:1). And we have this encouragingly wonderful explanation in John's first letter. John writes 'I am writing to you so that you may not sin. But *if anyone does sin,* we have an Advocate with the Father, Jesus Christ the righteous, and He is the expiation, the atoning sacrifice, for our sins'. (I John 2:1,2). We want to add a heartfelt, 'thanks be to God' for this provision of His grace.

Paul is grateful to be able to say that through the law, the law which gave him the knowledge of sin (Romans 7:7), he died to the law. Though he never not commits sin, sin no longer has dominion over him for he is not under the law but under grace. (Romans 6:14).

He *died* to the law that he might live unto God. *He knew the operation of the cross in his life. He says, I have been crucified with Christ.* Through the cross he had come into such a relationship with Christ that he had completely identified with the cross. His life now carries the identification of himself with his Lord. His statement of belief is 'I have been crucified with Christ and it is no longer I but Christ who lives in me, and the life I now live, I live by faith in the Son of God, who loved me and gave Himself for me'. (Galatians 2:20).

He is not of course claiming any ability to take upon himself the sin of the whole world, as Jesus, his Redeemer, had done. But he was claiming that the cross of Christ was a tremendously powerful instrument in his life.

In His wisdom God had allowed an evil, barbaric, wicked method of torture and execution to become the means whereby all that is evil and wicked in the lives of men and women can be dealt with and exterminated. The cross was the power of God unto salvation. (Romans 1:16). It was the power of God and the wisdom of God (1 Corinthians 1:24) for though it was weakness to the Jews, a scandal to them that anyone who purported to be their Messiah should hang upon a cross; and it was foolishness to the Greeks, for none of their gods died in such a way, the weakness of God is stronger than men, and the foolishness of God is wiser than men. (1 Corinthians 2:22-25).

And in that power, Christ crucified had become Paul's whole life. He says, 'It is no longer I who live, but Christ living in me'. (Galatians 2:20). Christ crucified dwelling in me and I in Him. If I depend on the works of the law, I nullify, make of no effect the grace of God. If I had to rely on the works of the law for my righteousness, my justification, then Christ died to no purpose. (Galatians 2:21).

Paul knows the joy of being identified with Christ, first the power of the cross of Christ actively at work to bring him to faith, and then to be the source of the life within him, his wisdom, his righteousness, his sanctification, his redemption. (1 Corinthians 1:30-32).

No one can earn redemption. But what a relief to cast ourselves into the mighty embrace of the one 'who loved me and gave Himself for me' (Galatians 2:20). Paul is very personal but the truth is there for all to discover. It seems that both in Antioch and Jerusalem, some had tried to come to salvation by observing the law. It is not 'try' but 'trust'. We cannot come by law, by trying, but only by grace. No one can please God by his or her own efforts. Paul had tried and signally failed. He had given up trying and abandoned himself to the cross of Christ, and to the Christ of the cross, to receive love and mercy and forgiveness and peace in his heart, for Christ had done for him what he could never do for himself, brought him near to a Holy God.

But now, for him to live is Christ. (Philippians 1:21). He will not nullify the grace of God by believing that the cross of Christ was inadequate, that something like circumcision was necessary because the cross was ineffectual. This is why the letter to the Galatians is so vehement. How was it possible that anyone could take that viewpoint, not only nullifying the precious gift of the grace of God in salvation, for the cross was an expression of

His utmost grace and generosity to sinful men and women, but also nullifying the gift of the transformation of life bought for us at such tremendous cost on the cross of the Lord Jesus.

Paul could understand why such an apparently trivial and mundane matter as with whom you take your meals is actually a behaviour with serious consequences. It determines whether the church is united or divided; whether believers are trusting in the cross of Christ for their salvation and their walk of faith in Him, or in something additional which they can do for themselves; whether they are trusting in the price paid by Jesus on the cross for their redemption or on their own ability to present themselves before a Holy God.

Paul's absolute conviction is that if justification is by the law, by the works of our own hands, then Christ died for no purpose. Justification is to Paul the truth of the gospel. It is the beginning of new life in Christ. The false brethren would want to introduce an alternative gospel, an adaptation of the gospel of truth as they travel between Antioch, Jerusalem or Galatia, and would deliberately or inadvertently make the cross of Christ of none effect. Paul has much to say about their past and present experience to the Galatian believers, and this he goes on to explain in chapters three and four.

Galatians Chapter 3

Galatians 3:1-5. The argument for faith over law

O foolish Galatians, who has bewitched you before whose eyes Jesus Christ was publicly portrayed as crucified? Let me ask you only this. Did you receive the Spirit by works of the law or by hearing with faith? Are you so foolish? Having begun with the Spirit, are you now ending with the flesh? Did you experience so many things in vain?--if it really is in vain. Does He who supplies the Spirit to you and works miracles among you do so by works of the Law or by hearing with faith? (Galatians 3:1-5).

Paul writes, having begun in the Spirit, are you now ending with the flesh? By being set free from the curse of keeping the law, the Galatian Christians have discovered new life in Christ. Before they came to Christ, however hard they tried to keep every aspect of the law, they failed. But being justified by faith in Christ, being made righteous not by keeping the law but by what Christ has accomplished on the cross, they no longer needed to rely on their own ability to keep the law. They trusted in His finished work of transferring His righteousness to them.

By the power of what God did for them on the cross of Jesus, they are set free from having to obey the law in order to achieve the righteousness which enables them to approach a holy God. All our sin, all that which separated us from God was dealt with on the cross, when the Lord laid on Jesus the iniquity of us all and carried it down into death. (Isaiah 53:6).

Now His righteousness, the righteousness of One who had never sinned (Hebrews 4:15), has been given to all believers. It is His gift to them, won for them at such great expense on the cross, setting men and women free from the burden of keeping the law. Now when God looks at those who have committed their lives to Him, He sees His Son, because they are clothed in His Son's righteousness. Paul says, we are reconciled to God by the death of His Son. (Romans 5:10).

O foolish Galatians says Paul. You know all this. This has been your past and your present experience. Jesus was publicly portrayed as crucified among you, displayed like a placard, a poster, an advertisement in public places and you responded to Him. Who has convinced you otherwise of the truth which you so gratefully received? Who has deceived you?

Galatia, as we have noted, was not just a city like Philippi or Corinth. It was a group of cities in a specific province. The church in Philippi may have retained a fairly consistent, family-based membership of Philippian Christians while adding to their number as the gospel went forward. But it appears that in Galatia, there had been much more interaction between the churches of Pisidian Antioch, Iconium, Derbe and Lystra. It would have been a matter of public importance that the gospel which was being preached among them, the gospel of Christ crucified, should be more publicly displayed. Just as Paul did later in Corinth, Paul and Barnabas went among the cities of Galatia, resolved to know nothing among them but Jesus Christ and Him crucified. (I Corinthians 2:2). The cross of Christ was absolutely central to their message. It was the truth of the gospel. (Galatians 2:5,14).

Paul had preached in the synagogue of Antioch in Pisidia, the Galatian Antioch, about the Lord Jesus being taken down from the Tree, that is, the cross, and laid in a tomb, from which God had raised Him from the dead and that through this Man, forgiveness of sins is proclaimed to them. And by Him, everyone who believes is freed from everything from which they could not be freed by the law of Moses (Acts 13:29,38). Paul's preaching on that occasion had caused many Jews and converts to Judaism to follow Paul and Barnabas, who spoke to them and urged them to continue in the grace of God. (Acts 13:43). The Gentiles too when they heard this were glad and glorified the word of God, and as many as were ordained to eternal life believed. (Acts 13:48). And the word of the Lord spread throughout that region. (Acts 13:49).

This ministry continued throughout Galatia. Paul and Barnabas went on from Antioch in Pisidia to Iconium, (Acts 13:51), Lystra and Derbe (Acts 14:6), preaching in such a way that a great company believed, both of Jews and Greeks. (Acts 14:1).

When they had preached the gospel in Derbe, and made many disciples, they returned to Lystra, Iconium and Antioch, presumably in reverse order, strengthening the souls of the disciples, exhorting them to continue in the faith and saying that through many tribulations we must enter the kingdom of God. And when they had appointed elders in every church, with prayer and fasting, they committed them to the Lord in whom they believed. (Acts 14:21-23).

This was the church in Galatia. These were the Galatian believers who, like the Thessalonians, and the Corinthians had turned from idols to serve the living God. (1 Thessalonians 1:9-10; 1 Corinthians 12:2). Idols of self-righteousness, of misunderstanding the prophecies of the word of God, as well as the idols of the Greek and Roman gods which were displayed all around them, and to which Paul and Barnabas had been likened, the crowds beginning to call Barnabas Zeus, or Jupiter, because he was the chief speaker, and Paul they called Hermes or Mercury. (Acts 14:12).

These Galatian believers had turned from all that was temporal, unsatisfying, life-denying, to the living, life-giving God. They had received the Holy Spirit by the hearing of faith. (Galatians 3:2). Paul is ashamed of their foolishness. Having begun in the Spirit, are they now ending in the flesh? (Galatians 3:2,3). Being concerned with other things like circumcision and table fellowship?

Paul says, 'Does He who supplies the Spirit to you, the Lord Jesus, and works miracles among you, does He do it by the works of the law or by the hearing of faith? (Galatians 3:5).

Paul recognizes that within their previous experience they had suffered many things. (Galatians 3:4). Paul does not specify what those sufferings were, but in every one of his evangelistic missions, there was opposition from those who rejected his message, and it could have been no less for the Galatian believers after he and Barnabas had left Galatia to return to Antioch in Syria. (Acts 14:26). Paul comments, 'Did you suffer in vain? If it really was in vain'. (Galatians 3:4). If the gospel which he had preached to them caused them to experience no change in their lives, why did they need to suffer? There would have been no opposition, no antagonism. All would have gone on as before. But what they had suffered was not in vain. There are promises attached to suffering

Suffering for Christians always has about it the element of suffering for the sake of Jesus. They suffer with Him, knowing that He suffers with them. They lean on Him, committing their suffering to His perfect will. They are identified with Him, and they know and believe that if they suffer with Him, they will also be glorified with Him, for the sufferings of this present world are not worthy to be compared with the glory that is to be revealed to us, the revelation of the glorious liberty of the children of God when Christ will be all in all. (Romans 8:18,21). So many have walked through the valley of the shadow of death with their Shepherd, knowing that He is with them, comforting them and bringing them to the other end of the valley, for it has both an entrance and an exit. (Psalm 23:4). We do not live in it. We walk through it with Him.

Suffering was not in vain for the Galatian believers. It was bringing them into spiritual maturity. The Holy Spirit had moved among them. (Galatians 3:2). He had worked miracles among them and Paul implies that the Holy Spirit is still doing His work; not by their assisting Him by the works of the law but by the hearing of faith, their inner being becoming more attuned to Him and His further generating of their continuing faith.

These miracles are a testimony to their acceptance of the gospel. They were a feature of the life of the church, a church moving in the power of the Holy Spirit. It was inevitable that such an attack as that from the false brethren should be aimed at a church fully alive to the power of God among them; an attack aimed at limiting, if not destroying altogether, what God was doing in Galatia.

This was the challenge to the church. Works of law or faith? The law or the Spirit?

By the works of the law shall no man living be justified. (Galatians 2:16; Romans 3:20). The law of the Spirit of life has made me free from the law, the law of sin and death. (Romans 8:1).

These are alternatives, so clearly set out by Paul. For him, it has become increasingly obvious that the Holy Spirit displaces the law in the life of the believer. If as Christians, they are living according to the law, they are no longer allowing the Holy Spirit His place in their lives. Law or Spirit? The choice is theirs. But Paul is warning them of the consequences of their choice. It could be either life limiting or it could be life transforming, a life full of joy unspeakable and full of glory as the One whom they have never seen yet becomes for them the one whom they love, the one in whom they believe and rejoice. (1 Peter 1:8 K.J.V).

Galatians 3:6-9. The faith of Abraham

> *So then, does He who provides you with the Spirit and works miracles among you, do it by the works of the law or by the hearing of faith? For it is written, Abraham believed God and it was counted to him as righteousness. Therefore, be sure that it*

is those who are of faith who are sons of Abraham. (Galatians 3:5,6. N.A S.V).

No compromise is possible between the gospel of truth (Galatians 2:5,14), and the 'different' gospel of those who want to disturb the believers, distorting the gospel of Christ. (Galatians 1:7). The consequences of believing in either of these two ways of approaching God are diametrically opposed. But concerned as Paul was for the Galatian believers, he wants them to know that if they have made the wrong choice, there is reconciliation.

A very different situation evolved in Corinth but Paul's message was the same. 'We beseech you on behalf of Christ, be reconciled to God'. (2 Corinthians 5:21). 'For our sake He made Him to be sin who knew no sin, that we might become the righteousness of God in Him'. (2 Corinthians 5:16, 20). 'Working together with Him, we entreat you not to receive the grace of God in vain'. (2 Corinthians 6:2).

Though Paul was here writing to a different church with different problems, he could have written these words to the Galatians with just as much force behind them, and in his attempt to reconcile them, to bring them back to their beginnings, and to a faithful, merciful God, he reminds them of Abraham.

Not only was Abraham neither a Jew nor a Gentile, but God preached the gospel beforehand to Abraham saying, 'In you shall *all* the families of the earth be blessed'. (Galatians 3:8). It is men and women of faith who are sons and daughters of Abraham, who are blessed with Abraham who had faith. (Galatians 3:7,9). This is the gospel which God preached beforehand to Abraham, foreseeing that God would justify *all people, Jews and Gentiles, by faith, but only by faith. (Galatians 3:8).*

Stott comments that this was the only way, the way of faith, by which the Gentiles could inherit Abraham's blessing, because

Abraham was the father of the *Jewish* race. It is possible that the false brethren recommended circumcision to the Galatian Christians in the expectation that they too could become Abraham's children. Paul is saying that they are already Abraham's children, not by circumcision, but by faith, the same faith that faithful Abraham had; totally committed to the promise of God. (Stott p 54).

Paul had linked the experience of the Gentiles who had begun with the Holy Spirit (Galtians 3:3) with his own experience of receiving the revelation of Christ *to* him and *in* him, (Glatians 1:16), together with the experience of Abraham.

Just as the Galatians had believed God for their justification, being made righteous; just as Paul had known the revelation of the Lord Jesus to him; so Abraham had believed God, had trusted in His promise to him, had fully and completely entered into a life of dependence upon God, knowing that there was nothing he could do to implement God's promise and purpose in giving him a son, and make him the father of many nations, (Genesis 17:4), and that God would do it all. He was utterly dependent on God. This was his faith and God counted it to him for righteousness. (Genesis 15:6). Any other way of approaching God was pride, self-satisfaction, trying to please Him by human effort; and anathema to God.

Abraham was a man of faith, and it was counted to him for righteousness. (Galatians 3:6). And so marvellous was this faith in God's eyes that in His Son, in Christ Jesus the blessing of knowing God and being known of Him would descend upon the Gentiles, that they might receive the promise, the promise of the Holy Spirit, through faith. (Galatians 3:14).

Galatians 3:8,9. Faith the way of blessing

The scripture foreseeing that God would justify the Gentiles by faith, preached the gospel beforehand to Abraham saying,

'All the nations shall be blessed in you'. So then those who are of faith are blessed with faithful Abraham.

Paul is totally convinced that those who are of faith are the sons of Abraham, not because they can trace their ancestry to Abraham, but because of their faith. He says, 'Like Abraham you are justified, made righteous by faith, and those who are men and women of faith are blessed in the same way that Abraham was blessed, being justified in the sight of God and leading a life in close proximity to Him. (Galatians 3:9).

The gospel which God had announced to Abraham was 'that in you, (in Abraham), shall all the families of the earth be blessed'. The Galatians had come into that blessing. In response to Jesus Christ, who was publicly portrayed and placarded among them, (Galatians 3:1), they had enjoyed the blessing of those who believe together with believing Abraham. This was what the scripture, the word of God, had foretold. For this was in the purpose and foreknowledge of God; men and women coming to Him, a Holy God, not trusting in their own merits, their own righteousness, but in the finished work of His Son upon the cross. Paul speaks here of the foreknowledge of God since the time of Abraham; but God's intention to have a people for Himself went far back, further back even than Abraham, into the unknowable realms of eternity. In Ephesians we read that the God and Father of our Lord Jesus Christ, the Father of glory, has blessed us with every spiritual blessing in the heavenly places in Christ, even as He chose us in Him since before the foundation of the world, that we should be holy and blameless before Him. He *destined* us in love to be His sons and daughters through Jesus Christ. (Ephesians 1:2-5).

God did not merely anticipate the gospel. He provided for it. And His Son and the Holy Spirit were complicit in His wise design, even if for Christ it meant the humbling of Himself to death, even death on a cross. (Philippians 2:8).

Galatians 3:10. The blessing of Abraham

So you see that it is men of faith who are the sons of Abraham... that in Christ Jesus the blessing of Abraham might come upon the Gentiles, that we might receive the promise of the Spirit through faith. (Galatians 3:8,14).

The Galatians had begun in the Spirit. Were they now tempted to end with the flesh? (Galatians 3:4). In Paul's letters, the use of the word flesh, *sarx* (Gk) usually denotes human nature in its fallen degenerative state. Paul's insistent objective is that the Galatian Christians should not return to that state from which Christ had delivered them. This terrible antithesis between the degeneracy of 'the flesh' and the life liberating gift of the Holy Spirit must be challenged, for they are mutually exclusive.

These beloved believers have known the power of the Holy Spirit, and Paul will do all in his power, in his love and care for them to bring them back, to show them that the works of the law, the temptation to look to the flesh, will not bring them to what they truly want in their hearts, a living, daily, hourly, relationship with Christ; in fellowship with the One who redeemed them, the Lord Jesus Christ.

The blessing of Abraham came through Abraham's faith. But Abraham's faith was not simply, or only, a meritorious act of faith or even a series of acts of faith but a statement of the way he lived, in close dependent relationship with God. He lived in the state of being right with God because his every activity was based on his faith. There were exceptions to this in his life, but his return was always to the altar, to the place of penitence; the place of worship. (Genesis 12:10-20; 13:2,18).

This was what Paul wanted for the Galatian believers, not even just the preliminary act of faith, precious and necessary though that was, but an ongoing life of faith which he had described earlier was that to which he himself aspired; 'the life I now live, *I live by the faith of the Son of God* who loved me and gave Himself for me'. (Galatians 2:20). If the Galatians are relying, not on faith, but on the works of the law, they are under a curse, for 'it is written, cursed be everyone who does not abide by all things written in the law, to do them'. (Galatians 3:10). But through God's covenant with Abraham, the Galatian Christians could come into the blessing of Abraham, walking with God in faith.

But that did not mean that they had to be circumcised, for the covenant between God and Abraham in Genesis 15 preceded the circumcision of Abraham and his son Ishmael in Genesis 17. Paul is adamant. It was not necessary to be circumcised to become a child, a descendent of Abraham. It was through faith, through total dependence upon God that Abraham received justification. He believed God and it was counted to him as righteousness. (Galatians 3:6). Circumcision was the outward sign that the covenant between God and Abraham was ratified, not only with him but also his descendents, beginning with Ishmael. It was an everlasting covenant, a *promise to be God*, not only to Abraham but to his descendents after him.

Circumcision is a sign of the covenant between God and Abraham, (Genesis 17:11), and Hebrews comments, God is not ashamed to be called their God for He has prepared for them a city, (Hebrews 11:16), the new Jerusalem, for all who are in that new covenant which was ratified in Jesus. (Revelation 21:2).

Galatians 3:16-19. The Law given through Moses

Now the promises were made to Abraham and to his offspring. It does not say 'And to offsprings' *referring to many, but referring to* offspring, *which is Christ. This is what I mean: the law which came four hundred and thirty years afterwards does not annul a covenant previously ratified by God so as to make*

> *the promise void. For if inheritance is by the law, it is no longer of promise. But God gave it to Abraham by a promise. Why then the law? It was added because of transgressions, till the offspring should come to whom the promise was made.*

Four hundred and thirty years after Abraham came the law, mediated through Moses, a man of faith who lived close to God and to whom was given the task and the opportunity by God to take God's people out of slavery in Egypt to freedom in the promised land.

Because they were children, significantly so described as the children of Israel, God gave them many commands through Moses which would draw them to Him, until the time of the promise to Abraham should be fulfilled. (Galatians 3:18).

The promise to Abraham was not fulfilled in all Abraham's descendents but only in one descendent, Christ. The law which came by Moses did not annul the covenant which God had made with Abraham and through Abraham. It did not make the promise void (Galatians 3:17). The promise was the promise of God and could not be rendered obsolete. But the inheritance of the promise was not by the law *but by the Spirit,* and fulfilled through Abraham's descendent, Christ.

For Abraham, there was no law to keep. For the Jews of Paul's day, there was a law, devoutly kept by the Pharisees and religious leaders but not by the people of the land, the *am haaretz,* people who were considered to be accursed by the religious authorities because they did not know the law. (John 7:49. Cole p 38).

These Galatian Jews who had come to Christ did know the law and had struggled to keep it, and were going back to the struggle to try and keep it again. Paul has to remind them that they are more privileged than many of their fellow Jews who do not know the law. He has to say to them, 'You know the law but you cannot keep it'. But that is a greater curse, for all who rely on the law are under a curse, for it is written, cursed be everyone who does not abide by all the things written in the book of the law to do them. (Galatians 3:10).

Paul is quoting from the book of Deuteronomy where Moses is encouraging the people to serve the Lord with all their heart and with all their soul, (Deuteronomy 26:16) because they are a people for His own possession. God wants so much to bless them, His people, and has given them ways in which they can be obedient to Him, for that is the way of blessing. But they also had to know the ways in which they were not obedient. They had to learn that disobedience is sin.

God knows the end from the beginning. Because He is God, He knows the perils and difficulties of human life for He is omniscient, He knows all things. The obedience of faith means that they can trust Him to guide them when they cannot see the way ahead; to trust Him to supply all their needs. This was the way of blessing (Deuteronomy 28:2).

But they also had to understand that the curse, which is the serious lack of blessing, comes through disobedience. If they forsake the covenant which He had made with them on Mount Sinai, then they are forsaking Him. By forsaking Him and breaking the covenant they are endangering the relationship they have with God and must bear the consequences, for God cannot pass lightly over sin and disobedience.

Moses has set these alternatives before the people as recorded in Deuteronomy 27. Paul is also setting the alternatives before the Galatian believers and also like Moses providing encouragement, for he knows that if they return to the Lord with all their heart and with all their soul, He will restore them, their faithful God (Deuteronomy 30:2). God wanted them to obey His commandments and had provided for them a sacrificial system which would enable them to approach Him in holiness; their sins forgiven; a system predictive of the greater sacrifice of His Son on the altar of the cross. Men and women need the righteousness which only God can supply, and He supplies it through the poured out life of His Son on the cross, and which He allows them to appropriate through faith.

Paul is so certain of this. The principle of faith was expressed by the prophet Habakkuk years earlier when he said, 'He who is righteous through faith shall live', or alternatively, 'The just shall live by faith'. (Habakkuk 2:4; Romans 1:17; Galatians 3:11). When this principle is overridden, subsumed under the alternative principle of 'works of the law', God cannot but acknowledge the curse, the curse of a breakdown, a loss of fellowship with Him, for those who have decided to rely on their own ability to be righteous cannot come into the presence of a Holy God, trusting in their own merits, for they have none. All their righteousness is as filthy rags, like a polluted garment, in His sight. (Isaiah 64:6). But what a blessing when they recognize this, for then they can come in repentance to the precious cleansing blood of Jesus, to the Father who is waiting to be gracious to them.

Paul is making the point that to insist that these Gentile Christians need to be circumcised, or excluded from table fellowship, is actually *a breach of the covenant on which the law was founded*, and therefore to break that law, entails the curse of Deuteronomy. Dunn comments, And this curse falls not only on Jews but on Gentiles also if they attempt to reach a holy God through their own merits. The curse is on *all* who do not persevere in doing *everything* written in the book of the law. (Galatians 3:10. Dunn p 85).

This is universal condemnation. But in Romans we read that our gracious and faithful heavenly Father has consigned all men and women to disobedience that He might have mercy on all. (Romans 11:32). Even faith is the gift of God to us so that our salvation might be of grace and not of works, lest any man should boast. (Ephesians 2:3). And He has put His seal on us and given us the Holy Spirit as a guarantee, (2 Corinthians 1:22); the promise to Abraham fulfilled that we might receive the promise of the Spirit through faith. (Galatians 3:14).

Galatians 3:13. The curse of the law

Christ redeemed us from the curse of the law having become a curse for us, for it is written, 'Cursed be everyone who hangs on tree'; that in Christ Jesus the blessing of Abraham might come upon the Gentiles, that we might receive the promise of the Spirit through faith.

Christ was the only one who fully fulfilled all the law. (Matthew 5:17). And the only one to whom the curse could never be attributed, for He lived His life in total obedience to His heavenly Father. He said. 'I do always those things which please Him' (John 8:29). But it was in His Father's will that men and women should be redeemed from the curse of the law. (Galatians 3:13).

The law of Moses said, 'Cursed be everyone who hangs on a Tree'. (Deuteronomy 21:22). If a man has committed a crime punishable by death, he is put to death by hanging on a tree, but his body shall not remain all night upon the tree but shall be buried the same day. (Deuteronomy 21:20). So God allowed His Son to be hanged upon a tree, to become the curse, all undeserved, which was due to His people so that they could be redeemed from the law.

Hanging did not involve torture. It was a fairly merciful death and in Israel the hanging normally took place after death, perhaps as a deterrent, though in other societies hanging was usually of living men and impaling more often used. (Kung p 148; Bruce p 165). The prohibition against leaving the body on the tree overnight in Jewish law may explain why when Jesus was crucified, hanging upon a tree so that He could become the curse-bearer, (Acts 10:37), He was taken down and placed in the tomb of Joseph of Arimathea, a tomb in which no one had ever yet been laid, (Luke 23:53), on the same day on which He had been crucified, in accordance with Deuteronomy 21:20.

Christ had become not only our sin-bearer but our curse-bearer, though of course in essence they are identical. Christ had become a curse for us to redeem us from the curse of the law. (Galatians 3:12,13). We no longer need to feel that we have to display our credentials before God, to try to impress Him and win His favour by our deeds of righteousness. Jesus did not just neutralise the curse. He took it away. We are free from the curse of the law, the necessity of trying to obey the law. We are redeemed.

And Christ has restored the validity of the promise to Abraham given before the law came by Moses; the blessing of Abraham to all who believe, the promise of the Spirit through faith, (Galatians 3:14); the purpose for which we are redeemed, that we might live by the Spirit. (Galatians 5:25).

As we have noted, this was the scandal of the cross, the offence of the cross for the Jews, that their long-looked-for Messiah should have been crucified, should hang upon a cross, a tree. But how else could He have redeemed them, but by accepting vicariously, on their behalf, the punishment, the judgement that was their due? To endure that terrible separation from His heavenly Father which caused Him to cry out 'My God, My God, why have you forsaken Me'? (Mark 15:34). He was in the world and the world was made by Him and not even His own people recognized Him. But to as many as did receive Him, who believed on His Name, He gave the right to become the children of God. (John 1:10-12). There were many who could not equate the terrible death He died with what they interpreted from their scriptures. But there were many who did receive and believe and enter into the life eternal He came to give.

This had been the case in Galatia. Many of the Jews had followed Paul and Barnabas, eager to hear their every word, longing to hear the message of salvation through Jesus Christ which Paul and Barnabas had brought to them. (Acts 13:43). O foolish Galatians, says Paul, you are like silly children. Then you were satisfied with the great gift you had been given. But now you want something more, something extra, not realizing that what you have been given is the greatest gift of all and nothing extra will ever make it more desirable, but if possible will detract from it.

Paul thinks of a human example.'To give a human example brethren, (his affectionate way of addressing them), once someone has made a will, it cannot be annulled or added to once it has been ratified. (Galatians 3:15). So why do you not understand that a promise made by God cannot be annulled even after four hundred and thirty years, to the time of the giving of the law through Moses? This is your inheritance, waiting for you to inherit it. This is true of someone who has died. This is the inheritance which you have; you have inherited the promise of blessing made by God to Abraham and confirmed in Christ, the One who died, Abraham's descendent. It is the promise of the Spirit by faith.

The curse of the law came later, for there was no law under Abraham. It became operative as the opposite of the blessing which God so longed for His people to receive and was added because of transgressions until He should come to whom the promise had been made, the descendent of Abraham, Christ, (Galatians 3:19), the righteous Son of God through whom the blessing comes. The righteousness of God for unrighteous human beings by faith in him, imparted and maintained by the Holy Spirit.

Galatians 3:21,22. The purpose of the law

Is the law then against the promises of God? Certainly not! Never! For if a law had been given which could make alive, then righteousness would have been by the law. But the scripture consigned all things to sin, that what was promised to faith in Jesus Christ might be given to all who believe. (Galatians 3:21, 22).

Paul knew from his own experience how utterly impossible it is to keep the law. He describes in Romans 7: 7-12 how hard he had tried. But he says, if it had not been for the law we would not have known sin. The very commandment which promised life to him proved to be death. 'Sin, finding opportunity in the commandment deceived me, and by it, killed me'. (Romans 7:8).

But, he says, the law is holy and the commandment is holy and just and good. (Romans 7:12). It has to be for it came from God. So how did that which was holy bring death to him? It was sin. However much he tried he kept on disobeying the law, and disobedience is sin. The law showed him that sin was working death in him through what is good and holy and righteous. If it had not been for the law, he would never have known sin. (Romans 7:7).

But the most tremendous truth of all was that the scripture consigned all things to sin, so that what had been promised by faith in Jesus Christ could be appropriated by the believer. (Galatians 3:22). It was now possible to be righteous, not by obeying the law, but by faith. This was in fact the only way to be righteous, to be able to come before a Holy God, to receive righteousness as a gift by faith in Jesus. He who is righteous through faith shall live! (Galatians 3:11: Habakkuk 2:4).

Paul says, and it is a cry from one who wanted above all things to be a righteous man of God 'Who will deliver me from this body of death?'. And his response was one of utter thankfulness, 'I thank God through our Lord Jesus Christ'. (Romans 7:25).

Paul is not arguing that there is no place for the law. On the contrary, as in Romans 7 so in Galatians 3 he is grateful for the law, for without it he would not have known sin, nor come to lay the burden of his sin at the feet of Jesus.

At one time, there had been charges brought against Paul by Jews who were among the Jews in Jerusalem who claimed that Paul had preached that they should forsake the law of Moses and not circumcise their children. Because of this charge, James, the leader of the church in Jerusalem had recommended that Paul should take four (unidentified) men with him into the temple for purification, which Paul did, for it was important for him to retain fellowship with James and the church in Jerusalem, (Acts 21:7-26).

The charge against Paul had been that because of the gospel, there was no room for the law. Paul is denying this, denying that the gospel is antinomian, against the law. The law is part of God's historic plan. It was given to show the sinfulness of sin. All have sinned and fall short of the glory of God. (Romans 3:22). There is none righteous, no, not one. (Romans 3:10). There is a wide difference between any righteousness achieved by works of the law and the righteousness of God, the pure white light of His radiant holiness. Paul says in the Philippian letter, that any righteousness he achieved under the law he counted as worthless. He 'counted it but loss because of the surpassing worth of knowing Christ Jesus, my Lord'. (Philippians 3:8)

God is righteous. His law is righteous. But we cannot keep the law. We can only be justified, made righteous by trusting in His righteousness, by faith in Jesus, the only truly Righteous One. Obeying the law could never give us right standing with God even if it were possible to do so, for it would only give us human righteousness. For true righteousness, we can only rely on the gift of righteousness given to us by faith in Jesus.

Why then was the law given? It was given because before the law came, there was no moral incentive. The law functioned as a restraint on moral behaviour until faith came. "We were confined under the law, kept under the law until faith should be revealed, so that the law was our custodian until Christ came", to lead us to Christ. (Galatians 3:23).

The law was itself a gift from God. It demonstrated the character of God for it was a projection, maybe a limited projection, of who God is and why He required that His people should be holy, even as He is holy. (Leviticus 11:45).

In giving His people the law, God had given them a precious insight into Himself, and His will for them. By sending His Son, He had given them an even greater revelation of Himself and His purpose for their lives. Paul's conviction was that the law was our custodian, our protector, our guardian until Christ came. Men and women longed for righteousness, for a right standing with God, but they were helpless, like children in a schoolroom, under the control of a schoolmaster, the law. This was God's purpose for them, to enhance and increase the longing, the desire to come to Him and receive from Him by faith what they could not earn.

And now that faith has come, they are no longer children under the restraint of a custodian. They have become sons of God in Christ, inheriting the promise of Abraham. (Galatians 3:29).

The law was our schoolmaster to bring us to Christ. It was an indispensable part of God's plan for it paved the way to faith. This was its purpose. The child in the schoolroom has gained maturity, he is no longer under the restraint of the schoolmaster. All the restraining patterns and routines and traditions of his life are gone. He is now free to enjoy and appreciate the gift of faith which allows him the freedom not to submit to the yoke of slavery which the law had become. (Galatians 5:1).

Those who have been baptized into Christ have put on Christ, like putting on a beloved garment, laying aside their previous experience under the law, through the joy of baptism, (Galatians 3:27), the baptism which signifies that they have died to the law through Christ. They have died with Christ through the sacrament of baptism and have been raised by Him to newness of life, so that just as Christ was raised from death by the glory of the Father, so they might walk in newness of life, His life. They are not under law but under grace. (Romans 6:14).

And Paul adds, all those who have put on Christ, clothed themselves with Him, have become sons of God. 'There is neither Jew nor Greek, neither slave nor free, neither male or female, for you are all one in Christ Jesus'. (Galatians 3:28). 'And if you are Christ's then you are Abraham's descendents, heirs according to the promise of the Spirit through faith'. (Galatians 3:14).

How important it was for the Galatian believers to know that there is no longer any distinctiveness which divides them from each other. All the walls which separated them from each other have been destroyed, broken down. They were once separated from Christ, strangers to the covenant of promise, having no hope and without God in the world. But now, in Christ Jesus, these men and women who were far off are brought near by the blood of Christ. 'For He is our peace, who has broken down the wall of hostility by abolishing in His flesh the law of commandments and ordinances. (Ephesians 2:12, 15).

The promise to Abraham was confirmed by a covenant, and largely concerned inheritance, the inheritance to be received as a twofold blessing, justification by faith and the promise of the Spirit. Like all the Old Testament covenants, this covenant made by God between Him and His servant Abraham was a suzerainty covenant, a covenant made by a superior to an inferior, envisaged as a superior power like an emperor bringing a lesser power into a treaty with himself, promising protection in return for services rendered. It was a vassal treaty.

But in the case of the covenant which God made with Noah, with Abraham, and with Israel in the days of Moses; and with David, (Genesis 9:8-17; Genesis 15:18-21, 17:2-14; Exodus 19:5, 24:3-8,34; 2 Samuel 23:5; Isaiah 55:3), God kept both sides of the covenant. And for us there is a new covenant, foretold by Jeremiah, which is an eternal covenant, established in perpetuity, the new covenant in the blood of Jesus. (Jeremiah 31:31; Luke 22:20).

All these covenants are based, not on a feudalistic agreement, nor on a parity agreement between equals, which would be a contract, but on a strong personal relationship between God and those whom He loved. God's covenants with His people were also His promises to them. The letter to the Galatians is emphasizing that God's promise to Abraham was justification by faith and the promise of the Holy Spirit, validated by the faith of His people who were inheriting the promises; faith in Abraham's descendant, Jesus Christ. Not *descendents,* but *one descendent,* Jesus Christ. (Galatians 3:16).

And this promise was irrevocable because it was promised through Christ. All who receive Christ are included in the promised blessing, whether Jew or Greek, for Abraham was neither Jew nor Greek. If the inheritance had been by law, it would no longer have been by promise. It would have made the covenant of God with Abraham of none effect, (Galatians 3:18), rendering the Abrahamic covenant obsolete.

How important was this truth to those Galatian Christians who had been born as Gentiles; who had not lived under the law as had the Jewish Christians. Because it was by promise and not by law, they could enter into it by faith. If the inheritance was by law it would belong only to the people of the law. But because the promise was given *before the law, it could be theirs too. It belongs to all people of faith, those to whom the gift of faith has been given by the Holy Spirit.*

The purpose of the law was to bring men and women to Christ. (Galatians 3:24). God gave His covenant through Himself as both suzerain and intermediary for only He could fulfil both functions simultaneously. Abraham and Moses, though men of faith could not take on the enormous task of mediation, mediating the covenant to the people, for they were people of like passions as ourselves. Though Moses mediated the law, he could not mediate the promises, the promises of justification by faith and the gift of the Holy Spirit. Only God could do that.

Abraham and Moses were representative of all that God wanted for His people, but only God could do God's work until the Mediator came, Jesus Christ, His Son. In His Son, God provided and mediated between Himself and men and women, 'the Man Christ Jesus who gave Himself a ransom for all'. (1 Timothy 2:5,6). In giving His covenant to Abraham, God acted unilaterally, in grace. God promised and Abraham believed. (Bruce p 178). And the 'one God' of Galatians 3:20 is the God of both Jews and Greeks. They are divided by the law but brought together by the gospel.

The law is God's law. It cannot in principle be opposed to the gospel but it can be an instrument in His hands to protect and guide the child in the school room, shutting him up to the grace of God until released by the One who should come, Jesus Christ the righteous. Believing in Him, the 'children' are justified. Believing in Him, they have the promise of faith, the glorious presence of the Holy Spirit in their hearts and lives.

This is the mercy of God, consigning all to disobedience to the law that He might have mercy on all; shutting up everyone under sin, that the promise by faith in Jesus might be given to all who believe, (Romans 11:32; Galatians 3:22). The gospel age has come, the coming of faith; that which was in God's heart from the beginning of time, salvation history; and that which now operates in the experience of every believer.

No one is disqualified on the grounds of race, status or gender. There is neither Jew nor Greek, there is neither slave nor free, there is neither male nor female, for you are all one in Christ Jesus. (Galatians 3:28). Paul has reached the apex of his argument. The law, though good, could not impart life. Only God could do that and He chose to do it by faith. Paul had written in Galatians 2:19, 'I through the law died to the law that I might live to God', and there is a whole body of believers for whom this is also true. They have been set free from the law. They have died to it that they might live to God. They are all one in Christ Jesus.

These principles are revolutionary, not only for the Galatian Christians but for all Christian fellowships throughout the world, both then and now.

Galatians Chapter 4

Galatians 4:1-7. From child to son. Spiritual maturity

I mean that the heir, as long as he is a child, is no better than a slave, though he is the owner of the estate, but is under guardians and trustees until the date set by the father. So with us. When we were children we were slaves to the elemental spirits of the universe. But when the time came, God sent forth His Son, born of a woman, born under the law to redeem those who were under the law, that we might receive adoption as sons. (Galatians 4:1-5).

Paul now needs to elaborate on what he has said about inheritance. He says 'I mean that the heir, as long as he is a child, is no better than a slave' (Galatians 4:1). Though still comparing the child as he had done formerly, as an individual without any self-determination, comparing him with a person who is under the law, Paul has moved on from his former position.

Paul is speaking now, not of a child in the schoolroom, but of a child who is the heir to all his father's estates. But because he is a minor, he is still under the governorship of guardians and trustees, tutors, stewards, administrators. His life therefore is comparable to that of a slave. He has no rights, no ability to make his own decisions. He has to do as he is bidden to do. He has no freedom of action, just as slaves cannot act independently. This was the case until he came of age, at a time appointed by his father. In Roman times, this was usually at the age of twenty-five. (Bruce p 192).

Paul says, 'so with us'. (Galatians 4:3). When we were children, in our spiritual infancy, we were enslaved under our guardians and trustees. We were slaves to the elemental spirits of the universe.

There has been some discussion as to what Paul means by 'the elemental spirits of the universe'. Bruce describes them as the elements which make up the material world, *stoixeia,* (Gk), primary things, rudiments, elementary teaching or knowledge, which Bruce says, of course includes the law. (Bruce p 193). He refers to 'the first principles' of Hebrews 5:12, that which governed the thinking of an earlier people in an earlier age, the first principles belonging to *kyros,* (Gk), not *chronos* (Gk); season, not time. The Galatians had been slaves, children, to these first principles, these elemental spirits of the universe, (Galatians 4:3). Now the season for milk, according to Hebrews 5:13, the season for first principles, is over for these Galatians. As children they have lived on milk. Bruce quotes Hebrews 5:4. 'For everyone who lives on milk is unskilled in the way of righteousness, for he is a child. But solid food is for the mature, for those who have their faculties trained by practice to discern good from evil'.

They have moved on from elementary, rudimentary, undiscerning knowledge. They are no longer children or slaves.

Bruce has suggested that this would be the natural sense of the phrase 'elemental spirits of the universe' (Bruce p 193), though others have suggested that the phrase refers to the four elements of earth, air, fire and water, and the divinities which are said to control them, as in ancient mythologies. Or they could be the signs of the Zodiac which were thought to have a bearing on human life. Or the heavenly bodies, sun, moon and stars and a belief in astrology. They receive worship from those who are ignorant of God. But this could hardly be said of those Christians who come from a Jewish background, though there may have been among them those who were formerly pagan.

These issues are discussed at some length by Kung p 189-192; Cole p 159-160; Stott p 78; and Barclay p 38.

Stott helpfully asks, 'Can bondage to the law be equated to bondage by evil spirits? God intended the law to be an interim step in the justification, the being made righteous of men and women.' (Stott p 79). There are evil spirits that would use the law as a final step towards our condemnation. God meant the law to be a stepping stone onwards to liberty. Satan, the adversary of God, uses it as a way of deceiving men and women into supposing that there is no escape from its dreadful bondage. Stott believes that there is definitely some kind of spiritual warfare going on for the possession of men's and women's souls, to bring them into slavery.

But how was it possible that the Galatian Christians had formerly been in bondage like that? Paul had earlier observed that they were like children sitting in a classroom. And though of course children have no independence of their own, the image does not bear the force of them having been in bondage to elemental spirits, an almost terrifying prospect. Perhaps there is a case here for engaging with the thought of E.P. Sanders who understands these universal, all encompassing 'spirits' as Bruce does, as first principles, elementary principles seen as the inflexibility and universality of the *application* of the law; the unremittingness of sin and the ultimate universality of death, 'as in Adam all die'. (Romans 3:22; Romans 5:18; 1 Corinthians 15:22). (Bruce p 194).

And for this universal problem there is only one universal solution, salvation by faith, through grace, the deliverance of all those who all their lifetime had been subject to bondage. (Hebrews 2:15).

This had been the experience of the Galatian believers. They have moved on from first principles. They have been delivered from bondage to the law. They are neither children or slaves. They are sons and daughters of God by faith, through grace. (Ephesians 2:8). Paul writes, 'When the time had fully come, God sent forth His Son, born of a woman, born under the law, that we might receive the adoption as sons. And because you are sons, God has sent forth the Spirit of His Son into our hearts, crying 'Abba! Father!' (Galatians 4: 4-6). So through God you are no longer a slave but a son, and if a son, then an heir.

Galatians 4:7-11. Sons, not slaves

Therefore, you are no longer a slave but a son. And if a son then an heir through God. However, at that time when you did not know God, you were slaves to those which were by nature no gods. But now that you have come to know God or rather to be known of Him, how is it that you turn back again to the weak and worthless elemental things to which you desire to be enslaved all over again? (Galatians 4:7-9).

Paul's polemical point had been that the situation of men and women under the law was identical with that of being under the elemental spirits of the universe. But the Father had set a date. When the time had fully come, the *pleroma (Gk)*, the fullness of time, God sent forth His Son. This was the focal point of time, the epochal moment when all the retrospective and all the prospective activity of God, met. It was the meeting point of history; before Christ came, and after He had come, B.C. and A.D. At this point in time, God sent forth His Son, born of a woman, born under the law.

Why? So that men and women might receive adoption as sons.

This was the goal of reconciliation between God and men and women to which God was moving, reconciled to God through His Son, leading them into relationship with God as obedient sons to their heavenly Father. Those who were under the law have been redeemed so that they might receive adoption as sons. (Galatians 4:5). They are no longer children, they are sons. And because they are redeemed, and are now sons, they have the Holy Spirit, sent by God into their hearts, the

Spirit of His Son, crying Abba!, Father!. And not only are they sons, but they are heirs, inheritors of the double blessing, justification by faith and the promise of the Holy Spirit by faith.

This is the gospel. It begins with God and God's desire for a people, sons and daughters like His own glorious Son. It began in eternity, and moved through time, recruiting men and women to that same glorious truth that in Him and Him only was this life given, eternal life through faith; and is ever moving on into eternity when all things will be summed up in Christ, united under the Godhead, things in heaven and things on earth, God's plan for the fullness of time, the mystery of His will, the purpose which He set forth in Christ.

God did not create the world and then withdraw. He had a plan, the mystery hidden throughout the ages in God, who created all things; the mystery of the church, union with Christ, to whom believers come as a bride adorned for her Husband; His bride, His church. (Ephesians 5:32; Revelation 21: 2). That through the church which is His Body, the fullness of Him who fills all in all, might be manifested the wisdom of God, and that this wisdom might be made known to the principalities and powers in the heavenly places according to the eternal purpose of God which He realized in Christ Jesus our Lord. (Ephesians 1:10.23; Ephesians 3:9-11).

The whole of the eternal purpose of God was fulfilled in the Son of His love, through whom we have redemption, the forgiveness of our sins (Colossians 1:13,14); we who have inherited the promise of the Holy Spirit through whom we may cry, 'Abba!, Father! (Romans 8:15).

Galatians 4:1-11. Excursus: The nature of sonship

Through God you are no longer a slave but a son, and if a son, then an heir. (Galatians 4:7).

How amazing that the Lord Jesus should have given us the privilege of calling God 'our Father', of being able to pray in His Name to His Father and ours. (Matthew 6:9). This is the coherence of Paul's thought. The gospel, the eternal gospel, so immense, so vast in its conception, so gloriously available to all men and women everywhere, the word of faith preached by Paul and the early apostles, summed up in one word, 'Abba'. 'Father'. Believers are sons and daughters of the living God.

When men and women confess with their lips that Jesus is Lord and believe in their hearts that God has raised Him from the dead, they are saved, delivered and redeemed. For when they believe with all their heart that God raised Him from the dead, they are justified, and when they confess with their lips, they are saved. (Romans 10:8-10,13). Everyone who calls on the name of the Lord will be saved (Acts 2:21, 38) and may call God 'Father'.

And salvation, under an eternal, supernatural covenant, between God and those whom He has redeemed through His Son, is human in its effect. Through believing in Jesus, men and women are not only related to the eternal purpose of God, they are also related historically to all those who have gone before them in faith, and are related contemporaneously to one another. But above all, they are related to God as His child, His son, His daughter, His heir, as they live to serve the coming King, when every knee shall bow to Him, and every tongue confess that He is Lord, to the glory of God the Father (Phillipians 2:10-11).

This is what God has done. To Him, our lives are not insignificant human lives. They are part of His purpose. The letter to the Ephesians declares that we are chosen in Christ from before the foundation of the world. (Ephesians 1:4). In answer to the most basic of human questions 'Who am I?' Stott says 'I can say, in Christ I am a child of God. In Christ I am united to all the redeemed people of God, past, present and future. In Christ I find my rest. In Christ I come home'. (Stott, p 76).

Stott concludes, we cannot come to Christ to be justified before we have been to Moses to be condemned. But once we have been to Moses and acknowledged our sin, guilt and condemnation, we must not stay there, we must let Moses lead us to Christ. (Stott p 76).

When the fullness of time had come, God sent forth His Son, born of a woman, born under the law, to receive a human likeness, to partake of human nature. (Hebrews 2:14). He was born under the law, the law of sin and death (Romans 8:2) so that He might destroy him who had the power of sin and of death (Hebrews 2:14) and to redeem those who were under the law, to buy them back to God, redeeming them, ransoming them by the precious blood of His Son from the power of sin and death so that men and women might receive adoption as sons and daughters.

Redemption, adoption; this is what God has done for us through the offering up of His beloved Son upon the cross. The cross, the fulcrum of time. And the grace of our Lord Jesus Christ who though He was rich for our sakes became poor that we through His poverty might be made rich, might be made sons of God, God sending His Son to die for us and sending His Spirit to live in us. (2 Corinthians 8:9; Galatians 4:6).

Galatians 4:8-11. The threatened relapse into slavery

Formerly, when you did not know God, you were in bondage to beings that by nature are no gods. But now that you have come to know God, or rather to be known by God, how can you turn back again to the weak and beggarly elemental spirits whose slaves you want to be once more? You observe days and months and seasons and years! I am afraid I have laboured over you in vain. (Galatians 4:8-11).

Perhaps we have temporarily forgotten that Paul is writing a letter, a very human letter to his friends, his brothers and sisters in Christ, in Galatia, to warn them of the very real danger that potentially threatens them, the implication of the tremendous application to their lives of what he is writing to them.

He is reminding them of the vast expanse of the significance of the God of all creation, the eternal God whom they worship, reaching down into the daily lives of humble believers. But this is not a theological treatise. It is *an appeal* to the Galatians to live in the good of all that Christ has done for them.

They have come to know God, or rather to be known of Him. (Galatians 4:9). Why do they now want to turn back to the weak and beggarly elements which had formerly brought them into slavery? To observe days and months and seasons and years? Periods of time in contrast to what He has shown them is His *eternal* purpose for them? Who is known to them and always available to them? (Galatians 4:9,10). They are redeemed. They are adopted into the family of God and may call God 'Father'. They may have a personal relationship and communion with Him like a child to his father, Abba! Father! the word used affectionately in the family circle, expressing loving nearness to God and implicit trust in Him.

They are no longer slaves to sin. They are sons and daughters of the most High God. And because they are sons, because of this precious relationship with Him, God has sent His Spirit into their hearts, the Spirit of His Son. (Galatians 4:6).

But Paul is concerned. Are the false brethren of Galatians 2:4 introducing into the church not only food laws and circumcision, but also pagan festivals associated with horoscopes, engaging the weak, powerless and beggarly in the church with the worthless elemental spirits of which Paul had written in Galatians 4:3? These false brethren were bringing the believers again into bondage, into a slavery from which they had been set free. Even if it had been only the observation of the Jewish festivals; the days, months, seasons and years to which the Galatian believers had been encouraged to return, this was still another burden impossible to bear. It was a third demand after the other two demands of the food laws and circumcision. We can hear the urgency in Paul's voice, 'I am afraid for you!' (Galatians 4:11).

The Galatian Christians are in a very privileged position. They are people upon whom the end of the ages has come. (1 Corinthians 10:11). They are at the end of the cumulative process of all that God has been doing since the beginning of time and far, far back into the realms of eternity.

How important then that they should not turn back from the faithfulness of God, who would provide them with a way to escape if they were being tempted beyond their strength, that they might be able to bear it. (I Corinthians 10:13). The faithfulness of God to them is His provision for them, His guarantee that they can rely on Him to help them resist the temptations posed by idolatry, false gods, false spirits, false teaching, (from which even today's believers are not immune). They have an irresistible, inestimably faithful resource, a loving Heavenly Father who will never, ever, let them down, who will protect them from anything that would prevent them from enjoying their status as free men and women, while trusting in Him, yielding their lives to Him, having entered into such a loving faithful relationship with God the Father through His Son and through the operation of the Holy Spirit, who desires only that the Lord Jesus should be glorified. (John 16:14).

With Father, Son and Holy Spirit all of one mind, that of bringing many sons to glory, (Hebrews 2:10), Paul's labour among them, these precious believers, can surely not have been in vain, even though he could occasionally have been afraid for them. It is possible to have a 'servant faith', to serve God, to love Him and look to Him for guidance in daily Christian living. John Wesley is reputed to have said that before his conversion, he had even then the faith of a servant. But when his heart was 'strangely warmed', he had then not alone the faith of a servant, but the faith of a son (Wesley's Journal, London 1872. Quoted by Bruce p 200 and also by Stott p 88), illustrating how necessary it is that these beloved men and women for whom Christ died should also know from personal experience the sending of the Holy Spirit into their hearts by God, crying Abba!, Father!. For now they are not servants, not slaves but sons, not 'almost Christians', as described by Wesley, (Acts 26:28; Wesley), but sons and daughters of the living God.

Galatians 4:12-20. Paul's concern for the Galatian believers

Brethren, I beseech you, become as I am, for I have also become as you are. You did me no wrong; you know that it was because of a bodily ailment that that I preached the gospel to you at first and though my condition was a trial to you, you did not scorn or despise me but received me as an angel of God, as Christ Jesus. (Galatians 4:12-14).

Paul knows and they know that they are no longer slaves but sons by the instinctive cry of their hearts to their heavenly Father in every trivial, or indeed, major circumstance. Abba! Father! they cry, responding almost automatically as the Holy Spirit subconsciously assures them of their place in the Father's family; the cry of a child, but a child who is learning to be mature, learning the way of grace; following Jesus by faith.

Paul has been emphatic in his letter to them of more than the desirability, the absolute necessity of recognizing their sonship. His heart goes out to them. 'I beseech you brethren, I implore you, I beg you to become as I am, a son of God, daily experiencing His love and care for me as my Father. For I have become as you are, newly discovering ways of learning, like a child with his Father, finding a new way of living close to Him and also living close to you, my brethren, my beloved brothers and sisters'. (Galatians 4:12). For they have a history together. When Paul first visited them, he was suffering from an unspecified bodily ailment (Galatians 4:13). But they did him no wrong. Although his ailment was troubling him, it did not prevent him from preaching the gospel or prevent them from listening eagerly to the good news he was bringing them. And though his condition was a trial to them, they did not scorn or despise him but received him as an angel of God, as God's messenger to them, as though Christ Himself had come to them. (Galatians 4:14).

We have no reliable information as to what the bodily affliction, the infirmity of the flesh (K.J.V.) was. It has variously been assumed that it was the thorn in the flesh of 2 Corinthian 12:7. Or that Paul had contracted malaria in the lowlands of Pamphylia (Acts 13:13), on the way up to Pisidian Antioch, apparently a well known phenomenon. Or that he had something wrong with his eyes. (Galatians 4:15).

But Paul is concerned. He writes, 'what has become of the satisfaction, *makarion, blessing (Gk)* which you felt when I first came to you? Where is that sense of happiness, of congratulation? Why has it evaporated? For I bear you witness *martyron (Gk)*, I am willing to go into a witness box and swear, that if it were possible *dynaton (Gk),* if it were within your power, you would have given me your eyes to replace mine'. (Galatians 4:15).

At that time, they would have done everything possible to help him physically, as they were being blessed spiritually by what he was sharing with them. Of course, it may have been his eyes which were the bodily ailment of which he speaks. But what he is saying is rather more relevant, that no sacrifice on their part, even the sacrifice of their eyes would be too great a price to pay for the privilege of hearing the gospel. And that equally, no sacrifice on his part, even the (temporary) loss of his eyesight was too great, if it enabled them to receive the message, the truth of the gospel, and turn to Christ. He says 'My little children, with whom I am again in travail, suffering with the pain of childbirth, until Christ be formed in you!' (Galatians 4:19). The time of suffering for him had become a time of blessing for them, that time when Paul had first come to them with the gospel.

But Paul is again in travail, again suffering as women suffer the pain of childbirth because the situation has changed. It is a costly pathway, the pathway of the gospel, both when preached and when received. But like King David, Paul could say 'I will not render to the Lord that which costs me nothing' (2 Samuel 24:24).

Until now, there had been nothing but wholehearted affection between Paul and the Christians in Galatia. But now he senses a certain reserve towards him. They had been listening to these false brethren. (Galatians 2:4). They knew that Paul would not approve of the teaching of these people, but they were really interested in what they had to say. These false brethren had approached the believers with soft words and with flattery. (Galatians 4:7). They made much of them but to no good purpose, for their intention was to shut them out of fellowship with Paul. (Glatians 4:17). Had Paul become their enemy because he told them the truth? How could they even think of Paul as an enemy? He would have no problem with these false teachers if they simply encouraged the believers in their faith, but that had not been their intention. (Galatians 4:18). Their intention had been to subvert the gospel of truth brought to these precious men and women by Paul, the gospel of justification by faith alone, the gospel of being crucified with Christ so that Christ could dwell in their hearts by faith, so that they could be rooted and grounded in love, (Ephesians 3:17), so that the life they lived in the flesh, they could live by the faith of the Son of God who loved them and gave Himself for them. (Galatians 2:20).

O my little children! says Paul. If only I could be with you and change my tone, for I am perplexed about you. (Galatians 4:20). The letter is no substitute for being with them personally. If he was with them they would be able to see by his gestures, by the tone of his voice, by the expression on his face, how much he loved them, as a father loves his children. He does not want to be severe with them. He knows that cold, clinical examination of the argument when written down, cannot be the same as the warmth of the emotional presence of each to the other.

But he would be neglectful of his love for them if he allowed these considerations to get in the way of his needing to explain the serious consequences of the teaching of these false brethren, teaching that was bringing His beloved children again into spiritual bondage, a bondage from which they had been delivered, released by the power of the Holy Spirit through faith in Christ. (Galatians 2:14).

Galatians 4:12-31. The story of Hagar and Sarah

> *Tell me, you who desire to be under the law, do you not hear the law? For it is written that Abraham had two sons, one by a slave and one by a free woman. But the son of the slave woman was born according to the flesh, the son of the slave woman through promise. Now this is an allegory. These women are two covenants. One is from Mount Sinai, bearing children for slavery; she is Hagar. Now Hagar is Mount Sinai in Arabia. She corresponds to the present Jerusalem, for she is in slavery with her children. But the Jerusalem above is free, and she is our mother. (Galatians 4:21-26).*

Once again Paul turns to the Old Testament scriptures, to the story of Abraham and his two sons, Ishmael, the son of Sarah's handmaid Hagar, and Isaac, the son of Sarah, thirteen years later; to underline his point about the law. Paul interprets the story allegorically. (Galatians 4:24). The story itself is one of great sadness, but Paul understands it as conveying a great truth.

To be a barren woman at the time of Abraham and for many years subsequently was shameful, a great disgrace. In spite of what God had promised to Abraham, that He would make of him a great nation, and that through him all the families of the earth would be blessed, (Genesis 12:2,3), Sarah remained childless. Again, in Genesis 15:4, Abraham received the promise from God that his own son should be his heir. But still Sarah had no child. (Genesis 16:10). In desperation, and with the connivance of Abraham, Sarah gave her handmaid to Abraham so that he could have a son through Hagar. And in due time, Ishmael, meaning 'God hears', was born.

Abraham, as he then was, was eighty-six when Ishmael was born, and Abraham loved him. When he was ninety years old, God promised to give him a son with Sarah and when he was a hundred and Sarah was ninety, Isaac was born (Genesis 17:17). Abraham pleaded with God, 'O that Ishmael might live in your sight! Be accepted as the son of your servant!' (Genesis 17:18). But Ishmael had been born of the flesh, the fleshly desire of Sarah to try to implement God's purposes in her own way, with the full cooperation of her husband.

Isaac was the child of promise, God's promise to Abraham fulfilled. God had said to Abraham, 'As for Sarah your wife, I will bless her and moreover I will give you a son by her. I will bless her and she shall be the mother of many nations. (Genesis 17:15,16). God's promise to Abraham made all those years ago was about to be fulfilled. The Lord visited Sarah as He had promised and Sarah conceived and bore Abraham a son in his old age, at the time of which God had spoken to him in Genesis 18:14. God had said, 'Is anything too hard for the Lord? At the appointed time I will return to you in the spring, and Sarah shall have a son'.

And Abraham called the name of his son whom Sarah bore to him, Isaac, meaning 'laughter', for Sarah had said 'God has made me to laugh'. (Genesis 21:3,6).

There is much more to the story of Sarah and Hagar, Isaac and Ishmael, but Paul chooses this part of the patriarchal narrative to emphasise yet again the difference, in fact the incompatibility, of life under the law and the life of promise under the Spirit. The story of Isaac and Ishmael is bound up with the notion of inheritance. Abraham wanted to share that inheritance equally between two brothers, but God said 'no'. 'Sarah your wife will bear you a son and you shall call his name Isaac. I will establish my covenant *with him* as an everlasting covenant for his descendents after him. As for Ishmael, I will bless him and make him fruitful, but I will establish my covenant with Isaac'. (Genesis 17:19).

So Paul says to the Galatians, you desire to be under the law. But do you not understand the difference between law and promise? For it is written, Abraham had two sons, one by a slave and one by a free woman. But the son of the slave was born according to the flesh, and the son of the freewoman through promise. (Galatians 4:23).

Paul has moved from 'the flesh' to 'the law', and this may be incongruous because the law did not exist at the time of Abraham. But there is a congruity between flesh and law as interpreted by Paul. That which is born of the flesh is flesh. That which is born of the Spirit is spirit, (John 3:6), said Jesus. Flesh may of course mean the ordinary course of nature and no moral censure is implied. But it can also, in Paul's thought, be that which is opposed to the Spirit. The mind that is set on the flesh is hostile to God, it does not submit to God's law, indeed it cannot, and those who are in the flesh cannot please God. For those who set their minds on the flesh cannot live according to the Spirit. (Romans 8:5-8).

Paul later writes to the Philippians, 'Look out for those who would mutilate the flesh, those who want you to be circumcised. For we are the true circumcision, who worship God in the Spirit and glory in Christ Jesus and have no confidence in the flesh', (Philippians 3:2,3); using the concept of 'flesh' in both senses. Paul is even more specific in the Galatian letter when he makes a list of 'the works of the flesh', which are plain. (Galatians 5:19). It is noteworthy that all the works of the flesh which he enumerates are sin and therefore against the law, but actually are more of the display of a human attitude of rebellion against God. They have as their origin some kind of personal satisfaction or resentment against others or an impulse towards impurity.

This is therefore Paul's understanding of flesh in opposition to spirit. It is that state of a human being which is concerned with self, not with God, a self-gratification which may lead to sin, and is in fact rebellion against God. There is a kind of sphere of sin in which the unregenerate person lives. (E.P. Sanders. *Paul and Palestinian Judaism,* p 276). On this level of understanding, it is obvious that that which is of the flesh cannot please God. It is without faith, and without faith, it is impossible to please Him, for those who would come to Him must believe that He *is*, and that He is the rewarder of them who diligently seek after Him (Hebrews 11:6).

When Paul says that flesh and blood cannot inherit the kingdom of God, he has more than the natural man or woman in view. (1 Corinthians 15:50). There has to be a transformation, the inheritance of the Holy Spirit by faith. There has to a witness of the Holy Spirit that we are children of God, and if children, them heirs, heirs of God and joint heirs with Christ, inheriting all the blessings of being with Christ in the heavenly places, even as He chose us in Him from before the foundation of the world. (Romans 8:16; Ephesians 1:3,4).

This is Paul's wisdom regarding 'flesh'; not the natural life of that person, but their relation to that life, and how it affects their behaviour: while the life of faith is the inner life responding to the claims of God.

It is possible, even for a believer, to use the ordinary everyday claims of human existence, to live out a life which is not chiefly concerned with individual wants and desires or legitimate responsibilities, which does not deliberately crowd out the Holy Spirit, but yet through it all fails to live under His control and guidance. There may be no self-appraisal, no self-sufficiency which ignores the merciful provision of a generous God, no self-aggrandisement, and yet the person is not walking in the spirit but in the flesh. Paul does not want this for his beloved Galatian believers, as he makes clear in chapter 5. But neither does he want them to come under slavery to the law. He does not want them to gratify the desires of the flesh, but to live by the Spirit. (Galatians 5:17).

'Flesh,' *sarx'* (Gk), is defined by Bruce as used by Paul, not simply of weak human nature, nor yet of life under the *stoixeia*, the elementary first principles or spirits (Galatians 4:3,9), but life as *opposed* to life in the Spirit. It becomes a binary principle. Either a person is living in the flesh or living in the Spirit.

This may appear somewhat rigid. Perhaps we would like to think that here is a midway course, not being entirely in the Spirit but neither living in the flesh. But Bruce believes that for Paul, any life not lived in the spirit is life in the flesh. He claims that 'flesh' denotes that regarding element in human nature which has been corrupted at its source, with its appetites and propensities, and which if unchecked produces the works of the flesh listed in Galatians 5:17. (Bruce p 256). He describes that as 'unrestrained licence'.

Had the troublemakers who were exerting such influence in Corinth observed the danger of unrestrained licence, which was what they imagined the full salvation of which Paul preached could lead to, and considered that obedience to the law provided some protection against it? Paul could not agree with this point of view. The principle of law in any form he considered to be compatible with being in slavery to sin. Bruce comments, the law belongs to existence in the flesh and stimulates the very sin that it forbids. (Bruce p 240).

The answer to both law and flesh is walking in the Spirit, allowing the power of the cross of Christ to sever the relationship of the believer to the flesh even as it had already severed his relation to the law. Paul had already described this as his own experience in Galatians 3:19. He says,' I have been crucified with Christ. The power of the cross has been at work within me. His cross is actual in my life and it is no longer I but Christ who lives in me, and the life I now live, I live by the faith of the Son of God who loved me and gave Himself for me'.

Paul is declaring that the power of the cross is dealing with the flesh even as it had dealt with the law. He says, through the law which showed me what I was, I died to the law that I might live to God'. (Galatians 3:19). Do the believers truly want to live to God? Then they must die to the law.

The cross had been effective in releasing Paul from the law. He had reckoned himself to be dead to sin but alive to God through the death which Jesus died on the cross. (Romans 6:10,11). Jesus cancelled the bonds which stood against us with its legal demands. He set it aside, nailing it to His cross, disarming the principalities and powers, triumphing over them in the cross. (Colossians 2:14,15).

Because our life is now hid with Christ in God, we may put to death our members that are on earth, that which is earthly in us. (Colossians 3:5). Through the activity and power of the cross, the works of the flesh have been 'crucified' to us. Bruce says, the death of the flesh is the life of the Spirit. (Bruce p 257). There is power in the cross. There is power in the cleansing blood of the Lord Jesus. 'Tell me,' says Paul, 'you who desire to be under the law, do you really want to live under slavery?' (Galatians 4:25).

Paul does not want the Galatian believers to live according to the flesh, if that means living according to what they believe to be the best way for them to live, what they consider is best for them, but neither does he want them to come under a slavery to a set of commands and ordinances from which they had been delivered. What he calls an allegory when considering Hagar and Sarah, may also be seen as typology, a way of attempting to understand salvation history in terms of God working through people and events, to help His people discover the meaning and scope of His purpose, not only for them, but much wider, to all those who meditate on what He has promised, what He has performed and what He has accomplished.

Bruce helpfully gives examples of this typology. He quotes 1 Corinthians 5:17 where Paul writes, 'Christ our Passover lamb has been sacrificed for us'. The Passover lamb is a type of Christ.

Or how the glory of God, reflected in the face of Moses when he came down from Mount Sinai with the two tables of the law in his hand, is reflected in the more permanent glory of God in the face of Jesus Christ, and that we, 'with unveiled face', may share in that glory, as we are being changed from one degree of glory to another, for this comes from the Lord, the Spirit. (2 Corinthians 3:7-18. Bruce p 217).

The Old Covenant, conveyed to the people of Israel through Moses, entailed the keeping of the law; this covenant was so precious because it established them as unique to the only true God; that as a holy people they were completely the possession of a Holy God. And when Moses received the law, on behalf of the people, his face shone with the knowledge that these people belonged to none other than God Himself. When Moses received the tablets of stone from God to give to His people, his face shone.

But the people of Israel could not keep the law. It was external to them. It did not come from their hearts to obey the law, though they tried. It was a dispensation of condemnation although God had intended it as a dispensation of righteousness (2 Corinthians 2:9) by which they could come to Him. But because of the hardness of their hearts, (Hebrews 3:13), their disobedience and their unbelief (Hebrews 3:18,19) the Israelites could not enjoy all the benefits of the covenant which God had made with them. (2 Corinthians 3:14).

But where the Spirit of the Lord is, there is liberty. (2 Corinthians 3:14). The written code kills. They were not able to fulfil all its demands. But the Spirit gives life. (2 Corinthians 3:6). The Galatian believers have come under a New Covenant, ratified in the blood which Christ shed, and remembered in bread and wine. (Mark 14:24; Luke 22:20). This is the covenant which sets them free from the law of sin and death. (Romans 8:1). They are no longer under law but under grace, enjoying the fulfilment of the promise of the Holy Spirit.

Galatians Chapter 5

Galatians 5:1-12. Freedom in Christ

For freedom Christ has set us free; stand fast therefore and do not submit again to a yoke of slavery.

Now I, Paul, say to you that if you receive circumcision, Christ will be of no advantage to you. I testify again to every man who receives circumcision that he is bound to keep the whole law. You are severed from Christ, you who would be justified by the law, you have fallen away from grace. For through the Spirit, by faith, we wait for the hope of righteousness.

For in Christ Jesus, neither circumcision, nor uncircumcision is of any avail, but faith working through love. (Galatians 5:1-6).

Paul has already spelled out for the Galatian Christians in no uncertain terms the problems they would encounter if they took upon themselves the yoke of circumcision. But so concerned is he for their spiritual welfare, that he adds one last appeal to these beloved children of his (Galatians 4:19), one last warning of the consequences of submitting to circumcision.

'I testify again', he says, as strongly as if he were a witness in a court of law, indicating the seriousness of what he is saying. 'I testify again to every man who receives circumcision that he is bound to keep the whole law. *You are severed, you are cut off from Christ*, you who would be justified by law. You have fallen from grace, the grace of Christ who called you to Himself in the beginning. You are deserting the one who called you in the grace of Christ. (Galatians 5:3; 1:6).

Circumcision was only the beginning, the entry or introduction or initiation into the law. Once circumcised, the person was bound to keep the whole law. (Galatians 5:3). And Paul knows from experience that the law will become ever more oppressive and repressive.

Those among them who were Jews had already been in bondage to the law. Their slavery had been as complete as the slaves bought and sold in the market place who were utterly subject to the law and will of their master. The believers were used to seeing these transactions, some indeed may well have been slaves before receiving their manumission. If these beloved Galatian believers were circumcised, every action or reaction of theirs would in the future be determined by the law, that which had become their master. They would be bound hand and foot by it.

But for freedom Christ had set them free! They no longer had to submit to the law, Christ had redeemed them from slavery to the law. He had fully fulfilled the law. He is the *'telos' (Gk), the 'end' of the law for everyone who believes*, (Romans 10:4), so that everyone who has faith may be justified.

The law is holy and the commandment is holy and righteous and good, (Romans 7:12). Of course it is because it reflects the character of God. But it has been replaced by faith as the means whereby we may come to a Holy God, for it was through the law that men and women became aware of sin. Paul says, 'if it had not been for the law I would not have known sin'. (Romans 7:7). Then Christ came to him. The One who knew no sin had been made sin for him, for us, had taken that sin upon Himself, that he and we might become the righteousness of God in Him. (2 Corinthians 5:21).

Christ destroyed the power of sin, nailing it to His cross, (Colossians 2:14), *redeeming* men and women whether Jews or Gentiles, whether circumcised or uncircumcised, *buying them back to God* (which is what redemption means) from slavery to sin as a generous slave owner buys back slaves so that he can give them manumission, freedom. This is redemption. Men and women receive justification by faith in the redeeming blood of Jesus whom God set out to be the expiation, the propitiation, the atoning sacrifice for our sins. (Romans 3:24).

Redemption has been given to human beings as a gift. They could not earn it (Romans 3:24) but only gratefully receive it as a gift from the mighty hand of a merciful God who does not desire that any should perish, but that all may come to repentance and enter into eternal life. (1 Peter 3:9). Like Paul, we marvel again at what Christ accomplished on the cross for us, and we worship Him. (Galatians 6:14).

Paul is insistent. He says to the Galatians, 'Do not be yoked again to a yoke of slavery, a yoke which was removed from your shoulders at great cost by the death of Christ, like the heavy yoke removed from the shoulders of a weary team of oxen at the end of a long day of ploughing, that intolerable yoke, that burden from which Christ has delivered you, that yoke which Peter declared in Acts 15:10 that 'neither our fathers nor we have been able to bear'. (Galatians 5:2).

Do the Gentile Galatians really want to exchange what they have received by faith through the Holy Spirit, the hope of righteousness, (Galatians 5:5), for the dubious advantage of becoming like their Jewish 'brethren', their Jewish brothers and sisters in Christ; of being able to sit at table in fellowship with them, of being able to refute the charge of inferiority because they have not been circumcised?

Stott expresses it succinctly as a significant choice. He says, You cannot have it both ways. It is impossible to receive Christ, thereby acknowledging that you cannot save yourself, and then be circumcised, thereby claiming that you can. You cannot add circumcision, or anything else for that matter, to Christ, as necessary to salvation because Christ is sufficient for salvation in and of Himself. If you add anything to Christ you lose Christ. Salvation is in Christ alone by grace alone through faith alone. (Stott p 103).

If you receive circumcision Christ will be of no advantage to you for you will be relying entirely on your own effort at righteousness and not on the grace and forgiveness which comes from Christ, His love, His faithfulness His provision for all your needs of body, soul and spirit, the grace of Christ to which you have been called. (Galatians 1:6).

There is an implicit suggestion that not all, and perhaps, none of the Gentile Christians of Galatia, had yet actually taken the step of circumcision as advocated by the troublemakers of Galatians 2:4. Paul writes, "You who *would* be justified by the law", as if they were in the process of making up their minds, of being persuaded by 'he who is troubling you', (Galatians 5:10), as though their circumcision had not yet taken place but that Paul had heard from an unknown source about this danger to his beloved brothers and sisters and is doing all he can to prevent it. Paul says in Galatians 1:7, that 'there are some who trouble you and *want to pervert the gospel of Christ',* indicating intention, rather than result.

The subtlety of these troublemakers lay in this, that they had not made clear to the Galatian believers, that together with circumcision was included submission to the whole law. They had presented circumcision as just a token commitment, just some kind of initiation ceremony with perhaps the occasional observance of some days, and months and seasons and years (Galatians 4:9), a relatively small obstacle to be overcome in order to achieve acceptance in the community.

This may have been a small obstacle, but it was a huge mistake, tempting though it may have been. No wonder Paul says, 'I am afraid for you. I am afraid I have laboured over you in vain'. (Galatians 4:10).

There are 613 precepts of the law. (Bruce p 230). Did the Galatians not realize that every one of them had to be kept by the observant

Jew? No wonder that Paul had reminded them that all who rely on the law are under a curse, for it is written, 'Cursed be everyone who does not abide by all things written in the law to do them' (Galatians 3:10). God graciously gave to His people the Day of Atonement when typologically, all their sin could be carried away from them into the wilderness by the scapegoat. (Leviticus 16:10).

But even had they been able to keep all the law, It would not have brought them eternal life. That only comes through faith, faith in Christ. Seeking to establish their own righteousness would mean that they would not be seeking God's righteousness which only comes through Christ, the only one who is the fulfilment of the law. Grace and works are not considered as alternative roads to salvation. Justification can only come through Him. (E.P. Sanders, *Paul and Palestinian Judaism* p 297).

Circumcision, though only a minor surgical operation, means severance from Christ. This is the terrible consequence of wanting to be justified by the law. They would have fallen from grace (Galatians 5:4), from the precious privilege of relying on the undeserved riches of His presence with them, His love for them. If justification, being made righteous, could be achieved by the law, then Christ died to no purpose. He died in vain. (Galatians 2:21).

But we cannot believe that Jesus died in vain. The very suggestion that His death did *not* achieve God's purpose of creating a family of sons and daughters all like His own glorious Son, becoming like Him in every respect except in His deity, living in the mystery of 'Christ in you, the hope of glory', (Colossians 1:24), fills us with terror, with unspeakable fear, for if Christ did not die to save us from our sin, we are yet in our sin and have no right to come before a Holy God, no right to call Him 'Father'.

If Christ did not bear our sins in His Body on the tree, (1 Peter 2:24,25), we are still unconnected both to Him and to each other.

Our lives are in vain because we are chasing an ephemera which does not exist. With what relief and gratitude we can put our whole weight on these words, *'But God*, who is rich in mercy, out of the great love with which He loved us, even when we were dead in our trespasses and sins, has raised us up with Christ and made us alive together with Him.' (Ephesians 2:4).

Jesus did not die in vain. We are redeemed sinners, redeemed at the cost of His shed blood, saved by grace, by His immeasurable grace. (Ephesians 2:7)

This is the truth of the gospel. Paul says, 'You were running well. Who hindered you from not obeying the truth? This persuasion is not from Him who calls you'. (Galatians 5:7). Paul is bringing his argument down to a very personal level. He has made it clear to them that neither circumcision nor uncircumcision is of any avail, but only faith working through love. (Galatians 5:6). There is no righteousness to be found in either circumcision or uncircumcision but only through the righteousness which comes by faith, the righteousness which comes of faith in the risen Lord Jesus, faith which works through love; love to Him, love to one another.

Faith is the only way to fellowship with each other, whether Jews or Gentiles, the only way to peace with God and with each other through our Lord Jesus Christ. (Romans 5:1). Faith, not works, lest any man should boast. (Ephesians 2:9).

This faith has been gifted to these believers. (Ephesians 2:9). They have experienced the freedom which it gives them, the joy of freedom from slavery to sin by the power of the Holy Spirit within them. Paul knows that this is their settled position. And he knows that those who seek to unsettle them, whether one person or a group of people, will be judged, and will bear their judgement.

But there appears to be another problem. Paul is being accused of preaching circumcision. 'But if I, brethren,' he says, 'still preach circumcision, why am I persecuted?' (Galatians 5:11). Could it be that those who were trying to persuade Gentile Christians to be circumcised were claiming that Paul was of the same conviction, preaching circumcision because as a Jew he had been circumcised? He may well have preached circumcision to the persecuted believers after Stephen's death, and before his Damascus road experience, and if these troublemakers could claim that he was still preaching circumcision, it would lend legitimacy to their views.

But Paul perceives their inconsistency. If that were the case, if I were still preaching circumcision, why do the Jews still persecute me? Even though he is a Jew by nationality and background, like them, he is still being persecuted. So, he says to the believers, even if you are circumcised, that will not prevent you from being persecuted. Paul is being persecuted neither because he is circumcised or if he had not been circumcised. He is being persecuted because he preaches the cross of Christ, and that is a stumbling block to them, (Galatians 5:11), the scandal of the cross.

So it follows that whether a believer is circumcised or uncircumcised makes no difference. Either condition is equally valueless and totally irrelevant. What is important is faith working through love, (R.S.V.), faith expressing itself through love. (N.I.V.). (Galatians 5:6).

The faith which has become ours is no intellectual or cerebral event. It is a life-transforming response to all that God has done for us in Christ, the outworking of that righteousness which has become ours through faith. It is the fruit of the Spirit. (Galatians 5:22).

Galatians 5:11. The scandal of the cross

If I, brethren, still preach circumcision, why am I still persecuted? In that case, the stumbling block, (R.S.V.) the offence, (K.J.V.; N.I.V.) the skandalon, *(Gk) scandal, of the cross has been removed. (Galatians 5:11).*

Over against all that Paul has been saying of sin, of flesh, of law, he raises the vision of the cross as of two opposing realities. Christ has been crucified for us. This is the most tremendous event the world has ever known. For a human being to take his or her place alongside the cross, at the foot of the cross, by faith, is to declare that they are opposed to that other realm, the realm of sin and death; that other world and all that it represents, to glory only in the cross.

At the end of this letter, Paul writes, 'Far be it from me to glory except in the cross of the Lord Jesus Christ by whom the world has been crucified to me and I to the world'. (Galatians 6:14). On the one side, the cross. On the other side, the world, the principalities and powers which govern unregenerate mankind over which Christ has triumphed through the cross. (Colossians 2:13,14). The cross has become the locus of the authority of the risen Christ, the emblem of his headship, Head of the Body which is His church, (Ephesians 2:23). Those who love the cross hold fast to the Head, for there alone is peace, peace through the blood of His cross, (Colossians 1:20), reconciliation to God through the cross, bringing hostility to an end. (Ephesians 2:16). The gospel is the true preaching of the power of the cross of Christ (1 Corinthians 1:17) to those who are perishing. It is foolishness, folly to Gentiles, and a stumbling block, a scandal for Jews, but to those who are called, Christ crucified is the power of God and the wisdom of God. (1 Corinthians 1:23).

This is how God demonstrated His power and His wisdom. He allowed His Son to hang upon a cross. For the foolishness of God is wiser than men and the weakness of God is stronger than men. (1 Corinthians 1:25).

The cross is the dividing line between light and darkness, truth and deception, love and irreconcilability. Some prefer darkness, deception, hostility towards God and others. But others are grateful to be able to say, although the cross is a stumbling block, an offence to many, they have recognized the dividing line and have decided to know nothing but Jesus Christ and Him crucified. (1 Corinthians 2:2). Though the rulers of the world crucified the Lord of glory, (1 Corinthians 2:8), the cross had already been prepared by God before the world was, (1 Corinthians 2:7), so that His beloved children might receive, not the spirit of the world, but the Holy Spirit, the Spirit which is from God. (1 Corinthians 2:12).

This is the secret and hidden wisdom of God. (1 Corinthians 2:6). We are called by God to be crucified with Christ who was crucified for us. (1 Corinthians 1:26; 1:13). We have not understood a fraction of what it means to be a child of God, but we long to know more of what God wants to reveal to us through the Spirit. (1 Corinthians 2:10).

Thus, the cross is God's way of dealing with all that is against His Son. It deals with sin that is transgression against God; wrong actions, wrong decisions or attitudes that can only be dealt with by the sacrificial shedding of the blood of Jesus Christ upon the cross. It also deals with the enslavement to the power of sin from which men and women are set free by the death of Christ who was made sin for us, (2 Corinthians 5:21), who took the punishment for our sins upon Himself, became our substitute and died vicariously, in our stead, leading to our acquittal.

These are the subsitionary and sacrificial aspects of the death of Jesus. 'At the end of the age He appeared once to put away sin by the sacrifice of Himself'. (Hebrews 9:26). He died once for all, the righteous for the unrighteous, that He might bring us to God. (1 Peter 3:18). He laid down His life for us, in our place (1 John 3:16). This is the substitutionary aspect of His death. Both are supremely important. Jesus paid the price of sin for us who knew no sin, but who became sin for us, on our behalf taking our sin into death, death on a cross, that we might become the righteousness of God in Him, (2 Corinthians 5:21).

Galatians 5:11. The reason for the scandal of the cross

But I, brethren, if I still preach circumcision, why am I persecuted? Then the stumbling block, the scandal, of the cross has been abolished. (Galatians 5:11. N.A.S.B).

Paul has already written to the Galatian believers of the Lord Jesus Christ, who gave Himself for our sins to deliver us from this present evil age. (Galatians 1:4). But this was not Paul producing a doctrine of salvation. It was Paul living in the good of the power of the cross of Christ in his life, thankful to God for His great grace towards him, a man who had once persecuted the church, and was now determined to lift high the cross so that others too could come to the cross and find grace and mercy to help in time of need; the cross which had become God's throne of grace, where Jesus our great High Priest is always there, interceding for us. (Hebrews 4:16-25).

Some received Paul's message gladly. But for so many, this was a totally unacceptable message. Our generation is far removed from that brutal way of putting someone to death through crucifixion, though there have been equally merciless and cruel ways of imposing the death sentence.

In Paul's day, crucifixion was not only a cruel and horrific death. It was a scandal. Whatever reputation the person had had for the good works he may have done was utterly destroyed. He was humiliated, shamed, scorned, despised and made completely contemptible. It was a slow and lingering death, and perhaps more tragically, his innocent family shared the ignominy, the shame. Perhaps fortunately, the harsh, savage beating which the perpetrator of the crime often suffered before being hanged would often mean that they hung there in a state of torpor, or semi-consciousness. This was not the case with Jesus, who appeared to be all times aware of His Father until at the end He could say, 'Father, Into Thy hands I commend My spirit'. (Luke 23:46).

That this was a scandal, a stumbling block, was intensified for a Jew, for their scriptures said, 'Cursed is everyone who hangs on a tree'. (Deuteronomy 21:23). This curse was very real. It was the curse of being separated from God which Paul had identified in Galatians 3:13.

There was that moment when Christ hung on the tree, when the sin of the world was laid upon Him and He cried out to His Father, 'My God, My God, why have you forsaken Me?' (Mark 15:34; Matthew 27:46; Psalm 22:1). Why am I separated from you Father? It was the most terrible thing that could happen to Him, that He should be forsaken by His Father. But in bearing sin for our sakes, He was willing even for that. He took the curse upon Himself, redeeming men and women from the curse of the law, and is now enthroned on high at His Father's right hand. And those who trust in Him will never be separated from Him or His Father.

But for many Jews there was an additional problem. How could He be the promised, longed-for Messiah prophesied in their scripture? In those precious pages He was described as a future king, who would lead Israel back to the God of boundless mercy. They are His chosen people and He will deliver them from the tyranny of those who would do them harm.

How could this longed-for Messiah allow Himself to be hanged on a tree, dying a contemptible death, and be cursed? How then are all the prophecies to be fulfilled? Certainly not through this man who could not reign over them if he had allowed Himself to be crucified by Roman soldiers; who had ridden into Jerusalem, riding not on a warrior horse as He would have done if He was truly the Messiah, but on a donkey; whose followers appeared on the whole to be artisans, fishermen, the common ordinary people of the land.

To preach of a crucified Messiah was a stumbling block to any right-minded Jew. He was indeed crucified through weakness, and the Jews were unable to see that it was the weakness of God which is stronger than men, (1 Corinthians 1:25). And He lives through the power of God for He was raised from the dead by the glory of the Father (Romans 6:4). And those whose lives are hid with Christ in God are complete in Him (Colossians 3:3: 2:10. K.J.V.).

The one who had been hanged on a cross was being preached as being both Lord and Christ, (Acts 2:36), this one who had been crucified; and this to the Jews was intolerable. To the Gentiles, who when death occurred within the gods of their pantheons, died with a god-like death and who were now being assured that salvation depended on one who had no power to save Himself from a disreputable death, it was also a scandal, offensive, but ultimately folly, preeminently foolishness.

It is the cross itself which provokes hostility, and Him who hung there, not just the preaching of the cross. (Kung p 240). The power of God unto salvation is the weakness of a beaten, scorned and humiliated man upon a cross. That is God's power. His weakness is stronger than men. That is His foolishness, the foolishness which is wiser than men. (1 Corinthians 1:25). Perhaps Jesus could have died a sacrificial death in a more acceptable way? No. It was the wisdom of God that He should die publicly upon a cross. And who may doubt the wisdom of God? His will is always good and perfect and acceptable (Romans 12:2), and He calls us to abide in His will as we live the life of faith.

To nullify the scandal of the cross is to rob it of its saving power. (Bruce p 238). Bruce comments that all Christianity is contained in the cross. He quotes Denney, *The death of Christ,* p 152, as declaring that the cross is the generative principle of everything Christian in the life of man. To be shut up to receiving salvation from a crucified one is an affront to people's self-pride and self-esteem. People stumble because to come to the cross for forgiveness, for new life, is to humble oneself, to confess the need of something, Someone, outside of themselves.

To the Galatians, Paul is saying that there is no other way. These false brethren, secretly brought in (Galatians 2:4) to churches in Galatia as well as to the Jerusalem church, are seeking to encourage the Galatian believers to contribute something of their own to their salvation, just a small matter of being circumcised so that their self-esteem is kept intact. The cross is drastic, revolutionary, all-encompassing. It is the knife which heals. James and Peter both say, 'Humble yourself under the mighty hand of God and He will exalt you'. (James 4:19; 1 Peter 5:6,7).

Paul continues, 'I wish that they who trouble you would mutilate themselves'. (Galatians 5:12). He is almost reducing their approach to circumcision to self-mutilation. It may even be that those whom he calls troublemakers, who were advocating circumcision, had not yet themselves taken the step of circumcision. They were subverting the faith of the Galatian Christians while standing aside from their own teaching. Paul is convinced that 'those who trouble you, 'those who unsettle you, will receive the judgement of God'. (Galtians 5:10).

But as believers submit to the crucified Lord in faith, their old nature is crucified with Christ, they are dead in Him, but alive to God through the Lord Jesus Christ. (Romans 6:6-11). This is their freedom in Christ. Brethren, says Paul, you were called to freedom, that was your destiny in Christ. Do not forgo your freedom, do not use it as an opportunity for the flesh, but through love, serve one another. (Galatians 5:13). Be slaves of one another as together you seek the outworking of the cross in your lives, says Paul to his beloved brothers and sisters in Galatia.

Galatians 5:13-15. The way of love

For you were called to freedom, brethren, only do not use your freedom as an opportunity for the flesh, but through love be servants of one another. For the whole law is fulfilled in one word, you shall love your neighbour as yourself. But if you bite and devour one another, take heed that you are not consumed by one another. But I say, Walk by the Spirit and do not gratify desires of the flesh.

Though Paul is writing a letter and not a theological treatise, he has nevertheless given the Galatian believers all the theological reasons why they should pay no attention to the troublemakers; why they should shun their teaching; and the consequences of it in their lives if they accept it. But now he wants to pass over to the practical aspects of what he has shown them; what freedom from the law means in practice. For you were called to freedom my brothers and sisters, he says. Only do not use your freedom as an opportunity for the flesh, to gratify its demands, but *through love, serve one another*. You were called to freedom, freedom from the law. This is not just theoretical or an ideology to which you subscribe when you become a believer. You are genuinely free! Actually and in reality free! The law no longer has any jurisdiction over you.

But you do have a responsibility. Being free from the law does not mean that you can indulge yourselves, using your freedom to indulge the desires of the flesh. Your watchword has to be that through love you are servants one of another. You cannot do anything that would hurt another brother or sister or anyone else in any way.

The whole law is summed up in this, 'You shall love your neighbour as yourself'. (Leviticus 19:18). So you are free from the law, and at the same time obeying the spirit of the law if you love one another. Under the law you had a duty of obligation to love your neighbour. Now that you are free from the law you cannot help but love your neighbour, however the term neighbour is defined. The love of the Lord Jesus dwelling in you flows out to your neighbour. The law is fulfilled in you.

So Paul continues. Be careful not to snap at each other, be controversial or deliberately quarrelsome, or react to someone snapping at you. If you do that you will be consumed, made of little value as a follower of Christ. You will be walking in the flesh and not in the Spirit. But in summary Paul says, walk by the Spirit and do not gratify the desires of the flesh. (Galatians 5:16).

The Christian's sufficiency is in Christ, (2 Corinthians 3:5), and he or she is involved in the interdependent and loving fellowship of the people of Christ. (Bruce p 241). His or her only sufficiency is in Christ, and that is why it is incumbent upon them to walk in the Spirit. But this is the confidence which we have in Christ, says Paul. We cannot do it. We have no competence or the sufficiency to be ministers of the new covenant of love, but our sufficiency, our competence, is of God.

There is a sense in which all believers share in this ministry of loving because of the love of God which is poured into our hearts through the Holy Spirit who is given to us (Romans 5:5), so each believer may become a minister, not of a written code, but of the Spirit, for the written code kills, but the Spirit gives life. (2 Corinthians 3:6). Paul's advice is *apparently* so simple. Walk by the Spirit and you will not gratify the desires of the flesh. (Galatians 5:16).

The Galatian believers have freedom from sin, but not yet freedom from the flesh. That is the work of the cross in their lives. Through baptism the old nature has been crucified with Christ, buried with Him in baptism. (Romans 6:4). Through baptism, the believer has been united with Him in a death like His. (Romans 6:5). In that identification with Christ, he or she has been set free from sin, from the law. He or she is no longer enslaved to sin. It is evident that dead men can safely be said to be free from sin. The law of the Spirit of life, a truly alternative law, has set them free from the law of sin and death. (Romans 8:2). They are now free to serve, not in the old written code, but in the new life in the Spirit. (Romans 7:6). They have received the Spirit of sonship whereby we cry, 'Abba! Father!' And they do not need to fall back into fear; fear which is the characteristic of slavery.

While they were under the law, they walked according to the flesh. But now, they are delivered from the power of sin and they *may and can set* their minds on the things of the Spirit, not the things of the flesh (Romans 8:5) for the mind that is set on the flesh is hostile to God; those who are in the flesh cannot please God. But because they have become sons of God, both men and women, they can trust to be led by the Spirit. (Romans 8:14).

This is amazing to them. They want to be led by the Spirit and the Spirit wants to lead them. God has a plan for them. Once someone becomes a believer, this becomes his or her destiny, to be conformed to the image of God's dear Son, and this means allowing the Holy Spirit to deal with the flesh as they walk in Him. (Romans 8:29). And a glorious time is coming when we shall see Him and we will be like Him, for we shall see Him as He is. (1 John 3:2).

He will never allow anything to separate us from His love, (Romans 8:35), and because of His great love for His children, they are free to walk, not after the flesh but after the Spirit. They are now servants, slaves, of one another. Jesus said, 'By this shall all men know that you are My disciples if you have love one for another'. (John 13:35).

Esler suggests that they are now entering a new condition of slavery, of slavery to each other, mutual slavery, but that this a slavery based on love, the love of family members for each other. (Esler p. 217). They are in a state of liminality having crossed the line to join a new group and are in the process of internalizing the values expected of them. They have a new family. They are brothers because they have become children of God. (Galatians 3:26). But they need to learn as members of that family to live harmoniously. (Galatians 5:15). The works of the flesh are inimical to community life. (Esler pp 223-225).

This is not ethical teaching. Paul has already demonstrated that they cannot keep the law, so why impose upon them a second set of rules and regulations? Which they also could not keep? Christ humbled Himself and became obedient to death, even death on a cross, to release men and women from bondage to rules and regulations. (Philippians 2:8). The ethical code, the code written in the Pentateuch did not set them free. What they needed to do was to repent, be baptized in water and seek for baptism in the Holy Spirit, that which had been promised through Abraham long ago, that in Christ Jesus, the blessing of Abraham might come upon even the Gentiles, so that we might receive the promise of the Spirit through faith. (Galatians 3:14). 'You shall receive power when the Holy Spirit comes upon you', said Jesus to His disciples, 'and you will be witnesses to Me'. (Acts 1:8).

Paul says 'walk by the Spirit and you will not gratify the desires of the flesh'. So we need to define 'the flesh'. The flesh is that which opposes God. (Sanders, *Paul and Palestinian Judaism*. p 553). The flesh as defined by Paul is not simply weak human nature but is that self-regarding element in human nature which has been corrupted at its source with the appetites and propensities which if unchecked produces the works of the flesh. (Galatians 5:19). (Bruce p 240). The troublemakers of Galatians 2:4 would no doubt have considered that the most immediate way of dealing with the flesh would be subservience to the law. Paul repudiates that principle. Legal bondage and unrestrained licence are alike completely opposed to spiritual freedom.

Freedom is *in* the Spirit and *by* the Spirit. Only by yielding to the Spirit and walking by the Spirit could the flesh be dealt with, constrained, controlled, as the Holy Spirit lovingly uses the power of the cross in the life of the believer.

The desires of the flesh are against the Spirit. The desires of the Spirit are against the flesh. For these are opposed to each other to prevent you from doing what you would. (Galatians 5:17). Paul is explaining their own experience to them and he is saying that the answer is to allow oneself to be led by the Spirit for His leading will fulfill in us all the fruit of the Spirit, His indwelling in the life of the believer resulting in love, joy, peace, patience, kindness, goodness, faithfulness, gentleness, self-control. Jesus said, 'By their fruits you shall know them' (Matthew 7:16-20). All these, which are the characteristics of the Holy Spirit, all that defines Him, are made evident and available to those who are indwelt by Him and are led by Him. Let us walk in the Spirit, says Paul and we will not be carried away by the desires of the flesh.

This is the way of freedom, the way of love, the Spirit's way, Christ's way. The Galatian Christians had received the Holy Spirit by the hearing of faith. (Galatians 3:2). He had done miraculous works among them. They had received the promise of the Spirit through faith. (Galatians 3:14).

Bruce comments, (p 245), the believer is not the hapless battleground of two opposing forces. There is no reason why those who have been redeemed from bondage to the law should live any longer according to the law. They are not under law but under grace, (Romans 6:14), the grace of God, the gift of God, the Holy Spirit Himself. They have been called into the glorious liberty of the children of God (Romans 8:21), for where the Spirit of the Lord is, there is liberty. (2 Corinthians 3:18).

This is the privilege of those called out of slavery both to sin and to the flesh, into sonship, adopted into the family of God so that they can say, 'Abba! Father!', the Spirit Himself bearing witness with our spirit that we are children of God'. (Romans 8:10).

Galatians 5:16-25. Walking in the Spirit

But I say, walk in the Spirit and you will not gratify the desires of the flesh. For the desires of the flesh are against the Spirit and the desires of the Spirit are against the flesh, for these are opposed to each other to prevent you from doing what you would. But if you are led by the Spirit you are not under the law. Now the works of the flesh are plain which are these... (Galatians 5:16-19).

Paul evidently considers that a list of works of the flesh would be helpful to enable the Galatians to avoid them. Some of these, for example, fornication, *porneia (Gk),* and sexual irregularity in general, were common in Graeco-Roman society and considered as not particularly reprehensible. (Bruce p 247). The list includes impurity; the tendency to have such irregularities in one's thinking, even if not indulging them. Licentiousness, wantonness is also a form of promiscuity, throwing off all restraint, living blatantly without respect to others. (Galatians 6:19).

Idolatry is the worship of any substitute for the living God. Sorcery, *pharmeia,* (Gk), drugs, as in black magic, is the use of drugs in witchcraft. In itself, the word is neutral as in pharmacy, the dispensing of drugs for medical purposes, but Bruce says it acquired two pejorative senses; the use of drugs to poison people and its use in witchcraft. (Bruce p 247). This was a serious offence in Roman law. Its inclusion in Paul's list may indicate something of the religious environment in which the Galatians lived.

From sorcery, Paul goes on to enmity. Is it possible to compare sorcery with enmity? Surely sorcery is worse? No, says Paul. Enmity is itself a passion. It is hostility towards others on racial, political or religious grounds whether in the church or society.

It is the antithesis of love. Those who perform hostile acts or even hostile thoughts are allowing something poisonous to enter into their relationships. Enmity is a work of the flesh.

Strife may also come under this heading, for it is the antithesis of peace. Paul found strife in the church in Corinth, the quarrelsomeness that produces cliques, where one person will say, 'I belong to Paul', or another 'I belong to Apollos', or 'I belong to Cephas'. (1 Corinthians 1:11). It is malignant. It destroys peace between brothers and sisters.

Jealousy, *zeal* (Gk), may also be translated as the English zeal. It can be used in a good sense, a zeal for God, a divine jealousy such as Paul had for his beloved believers in Corinth who were being seduced away from devotion to Christ. (2 Corinthians 11:2). But It can also be used as that which stirs up resentment of another who is more successful, more distinguished, more wealthy or has something which the other does not. The love for one another which rejoices with those who rejoice and weeps with those who weep is the antidote to jealousy (Romans 12:15), and is of course a gift of the Spirit. (1 Corinthians 12:26).

Anger, an outburst of rage indicates a loss of self-control which is impervious to reason. The Greek word *thumoi* is the word for anger in Ephesians 4:26. Be angry and sin not. Let not the sun go down upon your wrath. There may be a righteous anger which does not lose its self-control, lose its temper. The word 'anger' has much in common with *orge, wrath,* and the remedy for both is, let not the sun go down upon your wrath.

In Romans 1:18, Paul speaks of the wrath of God against all ungodliness and wickedness of men. The wrath of God is not the irrational passion of anger; that would be anthropomorphic. The wrath of God is the beneficent constant pressure against evil. He does not protect men and women from the consequences of their wrong doing, because He has given them free will. But He is a faithful God who has provided them with His grace as a gift if they are willing to accept it, through the redemption which is in Christ Jesus. (Romans 3:3,24).

In Isaiah there is a description of God holding out His hands all day long to a rebellious people, who walk in a way that is not good. (Isaiah 65:2). God says, before they call I will answer. While they are yet speaking, I will hear. (Isaiah 65:24). God is a compassionate God, but there will come a day of wrath when God's righteous judgement will be revealed, (Romans 2:5), and for every human being who does evil, there will be tribulation and distress. (Romans 2:9).

Anger, wrath is a very serious 'work of the flesh'.

Selfishness, the next work of the flesh seems to be a minor problem when compared with immorality, but has something of the same origin for it puts one's own needs or desires before that of any competing claim, giving them the priority of importance.

This insidious work of the flesh may often appear to be justifiable on natural grounds such as health or personal security. But it displaces God in the thinking of the individual and certainly displaces the needs of others. He or she cannot look to the faithful provision of God as they daily walk with Him but are ambitious to show self importance, self-sufficiency and Paul says, self-gratification, a state of mind completely antithetical to the mind of Christ, which we have in the Holy Spirit (1 Corinthians 2:12,16), and antipathetic to the mind which was in Christ Jesus, who humbled Himself, emptied Himself, taking upon Himself the form of a servant, a slave, for our sake. (Philippians 2:5,7).

Paul moves on to dissension, divisiveness, that which promotes breakdown in personal relationships, the introduction of divisive teaching, anything which puts up a barrier between believers, especially between those who favour traditional ways of worship or behaviour, and those who are eager to try something new which they consider to be more enlightened.

Dissension is closely related to party spirit, the next work of the flesh on Paul's list. Party spirit, *airesis* (Gk), means *choice* and gives us our word 'heresy', alternative exegesis of the same text. The problem arises when one group believes one set of ideas, or doctrines, and another group cannot accept those ideas, but have ideas of their own. Some groups 'choose' one way of thinking; others, another way, leading to party spirit, to heresy, to factions within the church, partisan spirit, the formation of cliques. Orthodoxy teaches that there is only one way. Heresy indicates that there is a possibility of other interpretations.

When writing to the church in Corinth, Paul submits that there are factions, heresies among them but this may be helpful in establishing what is genuine. (1 Corinthians 11:18,19). But this is in the context of his absolute conviction that they need to come together, to partake of the Lord's Supper together. To be in Christ, to be led by the Spirit, abolishes all that would hinder them from coming together. (Galatians 5:20). There is turbulence in the church when each looks to his own interests and not to the interests of others. (Philippians 2:7,8).

The answer is to humble oneself, to become obedient to the working of the power of Christ in one's life, the working of the cross, the enabling of being 'crucified with Christ', as was Paul's experience, identifying with Him as the only one who can bring life out of death, righteousness out of rebellion. (Philippians 2:7,8; Galatians 2:20; 5:20).

Envy, the next work of the flesh, is related to jealousy, *zeal (Gk)*. But whereas jealousy may have a redeeming side, envy is wholly opposed to walking in the Holy Spirit. It is a grudging spirit that looks with envy on another's property, or peace of mind, or success. Such people do not love their neighbour, but despise him while wanting to have what he has. It is a complete lack of generosity of spirit and leads to bitterness, distrust and contempt of others. Like all works of the flesh, it begins with the self and ends up in opposition to the Holy Spirit of God.

Finally, Paul adds to this appalling list drunkenness and carousing. His problem is that people profess to know God, but deny Him by their deeds. They are corrupted and Paul recommends to Titus that he rebuke them sharply. (Titus 1:16).

In that culture, wine was usually mixed with a quantity of water, so to become drunk would indicate that it had been drunk to excess. Paul even recommends a little wine for a medical condition which Timothy apparently had. (1 Timothy 5:23). What Paul has in mind when speaking of the works of the flesh is drunkenness to excess, the kind of drinking that would lead in that society to drunken orgies, excessive indulgence in wine which leads to a weakening of self-control over both words and deeds and a disinclination to understand what God is doing through His Spirit among them (1 Thessalonians 5:1-7), for they are living in the darkness and not in the light.

Paul says to the Thessalonian believers, those who sleep, sleep at night and those who get drunk are drunk at night. But we are not of the night but of the day'. (1 Thessalonians 5:7-8). Drunkenness weakens the vigilance necessary for the Christian's walk with God. Paul writes to the Ephesians 'do not get drunk with wine, for that is debauchery. But be filled with the Spirit'. (Ephesians 5:18). And as one drink often leads to another, some believers are total abstainers, as William Booth recommended to the soldiers of the Salvation Army.

Debauchery, dissipation, lack of rational or moral control; these are symptoms of the works of the flesh. Carousing, drunkenness, revelry, was often associated with too much wine, but in classical Greece would only suggest a celebration after someone had distinguished themselves in the Games, or some other successful achievement; but would almost always lead to people being far from sobriety.

Paul is not against celebration *per se,* but he is against doing anything which might cause a brother to stumble. (1 Corinthians

8:18). In Christ we are free, but we may not use our freedom to become a stumbling block to the weak. (1 Corinthians 8:9).

Paul has given us a list of 'the works of the flesh', but it is by no means exhaustive. It is not necessary to believe that the Corinthians had either in the past or in the present been guilty of such behaviour, and neither that the Roman-Graeco world in which they lived was constantly assaulted by such behaviour. Paul is making the necessary point that these works of the flesh are utterly opposed to the Spirit of Christ, who is the very essence of God, His intrinsic nature, He who differentiates God from everything that is not God. (Cole p 210). But Paul also wanted the Corinthians to understand, and to be aware that there is a strict line of demarcation, that those who do these things shall not inherit the kingdom of God. (Galatians 5:21).

Where then do his precious brothers and sisters stand in relation to the kingdom? They have entered the kingdom through penitence and faith. But there is a further joyful privilege open to believers, they will *inherit* the kingdom of God, in its fullness. They are heirs of God and joint heirs with Christ! Because they are God's children! (Romans 8:17). To forgo that privilege by indulging in the works of the flesh, to abandon all hope of seeing the glory that shall be revealed when the creation itself will be set free from its bondage to decay and the sons of God will be revealed, would be foolish indeed. (Romans 8:18-21). Having begun in the Spirit, do they now want to end in the flesh? (Galatians 3:3).

The present time cannot be compared with the glory that is to be revealed, when Christ shall take His power and reign. This is the heritage of God's people. This is why those who belong to Christ have crucified the flesh with its passions and desires. (Galatians 5:24). This is why they live *in* the Spirit and walk *by* the Spirit, because they want to see the ultimate vindication of Christ and His death on the cross for all mankind. They want to see Him magnified, glorified, reigning in love over His redeemed people, seated at His Father's right hand. This is how they produce, not the works of the flesh but the fruit of the Spirit, (again, not an exhaustive list), by living in the indwelling, energising, Holy Spirit.

If this is a second slavery as Esler suggests, what a joyful happy fulfilling slavery of which to be part.

Galatians 5:22-26. The fruit of the Spirit

But the fruit of the Spirit is love, joy, peace, patience, kindness, goodness, self-control; against such there is no law. And those who belong to Christ Jesus have crucified the flesh with its passions and desires.

If we live by the Spirit let us also walk by the Spirit. Let us have no conceit, no provoking one another, no envy of one another. (Galatians 5:22- 25).

Saint Augustine 354-430 A.D, sat under a fig tree in his garden in Milan and heard a voice saying, 'Tolle lege! Tolle lege!' Take up and read! According to Farrar, Augustine rushed back to where he had been sitting, and seizing the manuscript of Paul's letter to the Romans, he opened it and read, 'Let us cast off the works of darkness and put on the armour of light; let us conduct ourselves becomingly as in the day, not in revelling and drunkenness; not in debauchery and licentiousness; not on quarrelling and jealousy. But put on, clothe yourselves with the Lord Jesus Christ, and make no provision for the flesh, to gratify its desires'. (Romans 13:13,14).

In his 'Confessions' Augustine wrote, 'I wished to read no more. There was no need. For instantly, as though the light of salvation had been poured into my heart with the close of this sentence, all the darkness of my doubt fled away'.

He went to his mother Monica who had prayed for him for so long and told her of his conversion, and she recognized that

God had, in answer to her prayer, given her more than she had prayed for. (*The life of St. Augustine*. F.W, Farrar 1889. Edited by Robert Backhouse, 1993, pp 48,49). Farrar comments that the text was entirely misapplied from its original sense, p 42, which if true makes it an even more powerful act of God, that Augustine, on this verse of scripture; this portion of God's word, should come to penitence and faith.

We have every expectation that the Galatians had done the same and were now taking heed of Paul's warning; 'I warn you as I have warned you before that those who do such things shall not inherit the kingdom of God'. (Galatians 5:21). This warning was not given by some stern and autocratic figure, but by Paul, whom they knew and loved. They have as it were, received the first instalment, the down payment, the first fruits of the Holy Spirit, (Romans 8:23); the guarantee or deposit of the Holy Spirit in their hearts. (2 Corinthians 1:22). Now they can expect that as they walk in the Spirit, live their lives in the Spirit, He will produce in them the fruit of the Spirit; love, joy, peace, patience, kindness, faithfulness, gentleness, self control. 'Against such there is no law', says Paul (Galatians 5:22), as they continue to live in Him. (Galatians 5:25).

This is that to which His children are called. To live in the Spirit of Jesus who was led like a lamb to the slaughter and as a sheep that before her shearers was dumb, so He opened not His mouth, either in self-justification, self-vindication, explanation of His character, His origin and destiny or the condemnation of those who abused Him. It was the humility of One who made Himself of no reputation, who did not count equality with God a thing to be grasped but emptied Himself, taking upon Himself the form of a servant, a slave. (Philippians 2:5-8). He was the One who came, not to be served, but to serve, and to give His life a ransom for many. (Matthew 20:28).

This is the Spirit of Christ. This is the Holy Spirit and the fruit of the Spirit shows us dimly what it is to be like Jesus, that even when displayed through a human being gives us a faint reflection of Him, a mirror image of Jesus and His nature. What an amazing truth to lay hold of, that walking closely with the Holy Spirit will help us to become more like Jesus.

So we pray, let the beauty of the Lord our God be upon us, (Palm 90'17. K.J.V), the beauty of holiness, (Psalm 2:92; 96:9), so that the Lord shall greatly desire the beauty of His Bride, the church. (Psalm 45:11). For He has promised to give her beauty for ashes, the oil of joy for mourning, His garment of praise for the spirit of heaviness, (Isaiah 61:3. K.J.V), that He might be glorified, through the anointing of the Lord Jesus by the Holy Spirit. (Luke 4:18).

Why would believers any longer want to live by the spirit of the world when they may live by the Spirit which is from God, that they might understand the things which are freely given to them by God? (1 Corinthians 2:12). We thank God that through the cross of the Lord Jesus, the world is crucified to us and we to the world. (Galatians 6:14).

We assume that we recognize the *fruit of the Spirit* when we see it in others. But it is possible to simulate *spiritual gifts*; to prophesy falsely, to speak in a tongue which is not of the Spirit or give a false interpretation of a true tongue; to give a false word of knowledge or appear to work miracles. So perhaps the greatest gift of the Holy Spirit is the gift of discernment. (1 Corinthians 12:10). God does indeed bear witness by signs and wonders and by the gifts of the Holy Spirit distributed according to His will. (Hebrews 2:4). This had been the experience of the Galatians as Paul had reminded them in Galatians 3:5. The Lord had 'supplied the Spirit to them and worked miracles among them'.

But the gifts of the Spirit can be simulated while the fruit of the Spirit cannot.

In His first recorded discourse in Matthew's gospel, Jesus had warned His disciples that many would come in His Name and will say to Him on the Day of Judgement, 'Lord did we not prophesy in your Name? and cast out demons in your Name? and do many mighty works in your Name? And then will I declare to them, 'I never knew you. Depart from Me, you evildoers.' (Matthew 7:21-23).

But the fruit of the Spirit cannot be so adversely distinguished. It is difficult to manufacture love if one does not have it, or to manufacture joy or peace or patience or kindness. We are not born with these attributes though we may have an aptitude to learn them if we are given the opportunity, and there are many who would not claim to have had any spiritual experience, but who nevertheless have a real gentleness of spirit, an enviable disposition to loving one's neighbour. But whatever our earlier experience of life, coming to Christ, learning to live by the Spirit, learning to abide in Jesus who is the Vine of whom we are the branches, we shall bring forth fruit as He has promised, 'much fruit', which glorifies the Father and is proof that we are His disciples. (John 15:8).

This is the promise of Jesus to us. 'Abide in Me', He says 'and I in you. As the branch cannot bear fruit of itself, unless it abides in the Vine, no more can you unless you abide in Me'. As Paul acknowledges, this guards against self conceit, any provoking of one another, any envy of one another. (Galatians 5:26).

How can we have any pride or self-conceit in what we have genuinely become as we trust in Christ, since He has done it all in us? And we have only to look upon Him to see how far short of His love, His joy, His peace, we really are and how much further we have to go before that glorious time when He shall appear and *we shall be like Him,* for we shall see Him as He is. And everyone who has this hope purifies Himself even as He is pure, allowing the Holy Spirit to have His way in their lives. (1 John 3:2,3).

We may move seamlessly between Galatians, Hebrews, and the gospel and letters of John for all have the same message. God is looking for a people who will reflect back to Him the person of His own dear Son and it is to this end that He has given us His precious Holy Spirit to achieve that reflection, to accomplish that transformation. So we can comfort one another with these words (1 Thessalonians 4:18), for what God has promised, He is able also to perform, (Romans 4:21, K.J.V.) and we may trust Him fully.

The fruit of the Spirit is love, joy, peace, patience, kindness, goodness, faithfulness, gentleness, self-control. (Galatians 5:22). Is there a distinction here between personal and social identity? Do all believers equally display the fruits of the Spirit? We are not all alike. Everyone has his or her identity and yet, as we become closer to each other, and closer to the Holy Spirit, a group identity is formed. It was said of Peter and John that the religious authorities took knowledge of them, that they had been with Jesus. (Acts 4:13). What distinguishes the followers of Jesus is love. Jesus said, 'By this shall all men know that you are My disciples if you have love for one another'. (John 13:35).

This is unequivocally true. But if we refer back to the works of the flesh, (Galatians 6:19), it is fairly obvious that not all who live by the flesh are guilty of each one of the works of the flesh; guilty of all the same attitudes to behaviour as represented by Paul's list.

So we may extrapolate from that that it may be reasonable to suppose that the man or woman who is walking in the Spirit does not necessarily quickly or immediately learn from Him the value of self-control, or gentleness, for example. It may take some time! Fruit does not arrive spontaneously. It takes some time to ripen and mature.

Galatians 5:22. The preeminence of love

The fruit of the Spirit is love. (Galatians 5:22).

It is interesting that Glatians 5:22 uses the singular 'fruit' and not the plural, 'fruits' of the Spirit. This has led some interpreters of this letter to suggest that love is the fruit of the Spirit, and that all the other attributes are the result of the fruit of love in the life of the believer. From love flows all other aspects of life in the Spirit (Dunn p 112-114), as though love included all other fruit within itself. (Schweizer quoted by Kung p 272).

As we examine this suggestion one or two things become clear.

Firstly, Paul uses for love the Greek word *agape*, the love of God, His nature, 'the atmosphere in which believers conduct their lives'. (Kung p 263). In Ephesians 5:2, *agape* is the garment which they put on. In Colossians 3:14, *agape* is the motive of all their actions. In 1 Corinthians 16:14, *agape* love is the secret of unity. In Colossians 2:2, *agape* love begins with love for fellow Christians. In Ephesians 1:15, *agape* love includes church leaders. In 1 Thessalonians 5:13, *agape* love extends to all people. *Agape* love is the way to Christian maturity and is the ground of the Christian's appeal to one another (Philemon 5,7) and the proper restraint on the exercise of Christian liberty. (Galatians 5:13; Romans 14:15; I Corinthians 8:1,3).

This is of course only a selection of New Testament verses but it underlines Kung's claim that '*agape* is the atmosphere in which believers lived and still live'.

Secondly, there is also brotherly love in the New Testament, '*philadelphia*' *(Gk), (*Romans 12:1; 1 Thessalonians 4:9; Hebrews 13:1; 1 Peter 1:22); but the remaining words for love in classical Greek literature are not used in the New Testament, *eros* for sexual love and *storge,* affection, and sometimes the love of parents for their children. (Barclay p 54). When Paul says 'Love your wives', (Colossians 3:19), he is using *agape*, which puts a different construction on the relation between a husband and wife; that he should love her as God loves her, and that together, as two become one, they are demonstrating the love of God. *Eros* may endure for a night but *agape* comes in the morning for it has been there in the night too.

Christian fathers too may have more than affection for their children even in a society where children were not particularly worthy of understanding. The love of a Christian father for his children is based on *agape* love, so that they do not provoke their children in case they become discouraged, and the children are glad to obey their father because they know it pleases the Lord. (Colossians 3:20,21).

Is this idealistic life possible? Paul seems to think so. He says 'put on love, which binds everything together in perfect harmony'. (Colossians 2:14). Love is something we deliberately 'put on', clothe ourselves with. It is intentional. It is a matter of the will, not the emotions, and it is gifted to believers by the Holy Spirit who pours God's love into our hearts. (Romans 5:5). Their responsibility then is to receive it, to be open to the Holy Spirit, to bathe in His love, to know and understand that this precious gift of the love of God is transforming not only their lives but has an impact on others. They receive the Lord Jesus Christ, they receive His Spirit whom the Father has sent in His Name (John 14:26) and they receive His love into their hearts for He dwells with them and is in them. (John 14:17).

Jesus says that if we abide in His love, then His joy will also be in us (John 15:11) and we are justified in accepting that together with love, He will 'freely give us all things', freely, willingly, gratis, undeserved and without charge, (Romans 8:32, K.J.V.); may give us all things with Him. (R.S.V.). And may we not accept that this includes joy, peace, patience, kindness, goodness, faithfulness, gentleness, self control; a non-exhaustive list, for He gives us so much more than we can either ask or think by His power at work within us. (Ephesians 3:20).

Paul writes to the Ephesian Christians, 'I bow my knees before the Father... that He may grant you to be strengthened with might through His Spirit in the inner man; that Christ may dwell in your hearts through faith; that you, being rooted and grounded in love may have power to comprehend with all the saints what is the breadth and length and height and depth, and to know the love of Christ which passes knowledge, that you may be filled with all the fullness of God'. (Ephesians 3:14-19). Love is the way. Love is the only way. And this is Paul's prayer for them.

What a prayer that is! With its ultimate petition that the Christians of Ephesus would be filled with all the fullness of God. It seems unutterably impossible as we look at ourselves, but we look away to Jesus, the author, the originator of our faith. We consider Him and are content (Hebrews 12:2,3) for we know that nothing is impossible with God. There is no room for self-conceit, for the provoking of one another, for envying one another, (Galatians 5:26) for that is totally against what the Holy Spirit is doing in the lives of those who love Him. Paul has already assumed that those who belong to Jesus have crucified the flesh with its passions and desires. (Galatians 5:24). They have dared, (perhaps inadvertently, lacking the gospel of Luke), to respond to the invitation of Jesus to take up their cross and follow Him. Daily. (Luke 9:23).

Galatians 5:25,26. The two Jerusalems

Now Hagar is on Mount Sinai in Arabia. She corresponds with the present Jerusalem for she is in slavery with her children. But the Jerusalem above is free, and she is our mother. For it is written, Rejoice O barren one, one who does not bear. Break forth and shout, you who are not in travail, for the children of the desolate are many more than the children of she who is married. (Galatians 4:25-27).

Through reintroducing the allegory of Hagar and Sarah, Paul is insisting once again on the contrast between the law and the Spirit, spiritual bondage and spiritual freedom. The covenant between God and Abraham was founded on promise and the gospel was the fulfilment of that promise that in Abraham and Abraham's descendent, Jesus, all nations would be blessed, whether they were slaves or free, whether they were Jews or Greeks, whether having either Ishmael or Isaac as their ancestor, whether they are men or women.

They were blessed with faithful Abraham whether they were children of the free woman or the slave woman. But the son of Hagar was born 'according to the flesh'. This may simply mean that normal human procreation took place. But as we have seen, 'flesh' is often used by Paul for human life which is distorted by human desires which war against the Spirit and conclude by not obeying the law. This was how Ishmael was conceived. To be born 'according to the flesh' indicates a birth *opposed* to that human life which, though taking account of that which is natural, nevertheless walks according to the Spirit.

Paul is saying that it is possible to live a human life in the Spirit, relying on the power of the cross. And if a believer walks in the Spirit, he or she will not gratify the desires of the flesh. (Galatians 5:16).

Because Hagar's son was born according to the flesh, she is bearing children to slavery. (Galatians 4:23,24). In ancient times, if the mother was a slave wife, her children automatically became slaves, unless the free father acknowledged them as his sons and daughters. The Galatian Jews, like all Jews, prided themselves on being descendents of Abraham, but on being descendents of Abraham and Sarah, not Abraham and Hagar.

Paul is turning that comforting assumption on its head. He says Hagar represents the covenant made with God's people on Mount Sinai-Horeb, and which now corresponds to the present Jerusalem, the Jerusalem which the Jews know so well as the place of the temple and the sacrifices, the traditions and customs and history of their faith. But this Jerusalem is in slavery with her children. (Galatians 4:25). She is not free. She is under the covenant of law. If they are children of that Jerusalem which is represented by Hagar, they are under the law. But if they have been delivered from slavery to the law they are children of promise; they may receive the promise of the Spirit by faith. (Galatians 3:4). And they are then children of the new Jerusalem, the Jerusalm which is above.

John records an instance when the Jews said to Jesus, 'we are Abraham's descendents and therefore cannot be in bondage to any man'. (John 8:33,34). And Jesus replied, 'everyone who commits sin is a slave to sin. But if the Son makes you free, you will be free indeed'. They did not need the paternity of Abraham to declare themselves free. Jesus said they needed to be born again of the Spirit of God and then they would be free. (John 3:6). That which is born of the flesh is flesh. That which is born of the Spirit, and *only* that which is born of the Spirit, is spirit.

Because Hagar represents the covenant which God made with His people on Mount Sinai, a covenant based on law, and not on the covenant which God made with Abraham, the covenant of promise, these Galatian Jews must consider themselves to be children of Hagar and not of Sarah. Paul had already shown them that it is completely hopeless to try to win salvation by their own efforts, by their own merits, by trying to keep the law. Paul knew from experience how trying to keep the law is to enter an impossible state of bondage, of slavery to the law, captive to the law of sin which dwelled in his members. (Romans 7: 22,23). Hagar, the representative of the Sinaitic covenant, is still bearing children to slavery, the inevitable consequence of being unable to keep the law.

These Galatian Jews had prided themselves on being Abraham's descendents, but had perhaps given little thought to the possibility of having Hagar as their 'mother', always presuming that they followed Isaac's line. Paul's argument is that they are indeed Abraham's descendents, but they are descendents from Hagar who represents Mount Sinai, where the law was given, and are in bondage to that law until they come into the freedom of those who are the children of promise, as Isaac was promised to Abraham and Sarah, and as the Holy Spirit is promised through faith.

Hagar represents or corresponds to the present Jerusalem, the Jerusalem which for them is *now,* who is in bondage, in slavery, with her children, says Paul; but Sarah corresponds to the Jerusalem which is above which is our mother. (Galatians 4:24-26). Being a descendent of Abraham does not automatically convey citizenship of the new Jerusalem.

So Paul takes the narrative of Genesis and allegorizes it. Hagar and Sarah represent two covenants, the old covenant of the law, and the new covenant which Jesus has so powerfully claimed is the new covenant in His blood (Luke 22:20), the covenant which sets men and women free.

The Galatians, whether Jews or Gentiles are no longer under law but under grace. But this wonderful transformation has not come about by admitting that their Jewish faith had become what E.P. Sanders calls 'covenantal nomism', that is, the view that one's place in God's plan is established on the basis of the covenant, and that the covenant *'requires* as the proper response of man, his obedience to the commandments, thereby providing a means of atonement for transgression. (E.P. Sanders. *Paul and Palestinian Judaism* p 75).

Hans Kung describes this as 'merit theology'; as the condition of remaining in Judaism but which does not earn salvation. Either of these terms could describes the message which the 'troublemakers' (Galatians 5:12), are propounding as a way of living within the family of God.

Kung declares that what is really meant by the God of grace is that God, who is Himself living in the world; not discoverable and yet present; immanent and yet transcendent; here and now; close but distant; who precisely as holding, sustaining, encompassing, is always ahead of us in all life and movement, marching on and falling back, who precisely in what *He does not have to be but actually is*; who simply in His free grace according to the Bible is not the irrational but the reliable, steadfast, faithful God. (Kung p 168, 169. *Does God exist?*).

The grace of God, the provision of God, the Spirit of God, are all we need to live the life of liberty which He promised. Paul puts it rather more simply. He says, 'walk by the Spirit, and you will not carry out the desires of the flesh'. (Galatians 5:16).

All Jews believed that they were the descendents of Abraham, both historically and genealogically, but descendents of Isaac, whereas the Gentiles were descendents of Ishmael. Paul's objective in using the story of Hagar and Sarah, Isaac and Ishmael, was to show that this episode in Israel's history, rightly understood, concerns the antithesis of flesh to spirit, the antithetical covenants of free grace and law. God would, and indeed, did, bless Ishmael, but they were uncovenanted blessings, uncovenanted mercies. (Genesis 17:20,21).

This was what the troublemakers of Galatians 2:4 would have appealed to. The Gentile Christians could not be descendents of Abraham by Isaac because they were Gentiles. They could therefore not inherit all the blessings that came through the covenant with Moses on Mount Sinai, unless they were circumcised as Abraham was. (Genesis 17:24). Only by being circumcised could they align themselves with the Jewish Christians, descended from Abraham.

But Paul has inverted that distinction by saying that those who follow the law are children of Hagar whose son did not come into all the blessings of the covenant; the slave wife, who has birthed them into slavery. (Galatians 4:24). The children of the free woman, Sarah are those who know the reality of justification by faith; who have received the gospel; who are free.

This argument from Paul was not going to be accepted by the troublemakers of Galatians 2:4 but may have accomplished some re-examination of their faith on the part of the Galatians, both Jewish and Gentile Christians, as Paul contrasts the present Jerusalem to Mount Sinai, the place of slavery to the law, with the Jerusalem which is above and is free, which is our mother.

Paul amplifies the reference to Jerusalem by quoting Isaiah 54:1, interpreting Isaiah's prophetic witness to *the city of Jerusalem which had been left derelict* and bereft of her children who had been carried away into exile, into Babylon; *with the city whic*h *the Lord was going to restore and bless* and whose children would be numerous. This Jerusalem would be given the incentive to rejoice, 'Rejoice O barren one who did not bear, break forth into singing and cry aloud you who have not been in travail, for the children of the desolate one will be more than the children of her who is married. (Galatians 4:27).

Paul was probably using the Septuagint or Greek translation of the Hebrew Scriptures, so it reads slightly differently from the original Hebrew. This is a chapter full of promise and of the merciful compassion of the Lord for His people, of the remembered experience of His everlasting love for them and for their numerical expansion. 'And all your children shall be taught of the Lord and great shall be the peace of your children.' (Isaiah 54:13). Children were always important to God.

Paul understood the prophecy not just as being the promise of a restored Jerusalem after the exile, but as the founding of a new Jerusalem. With Isaiah's vision of foundations set in lapis lazuli, her pinnacles of agate, her gates of carbuncle and her walls of precious stones (Isaiah 54:11,12) the city is beginning to have the appearance of the heavenly Jerusalem of Revelation 21:15-21.

This is what God has in mind for His people. The promises of Isaiah 54 are understood by Paul to refer to the church, the new Jerusalem coming down out of heaven from God, prepared as a bride adorned for her husband (Revelation 21:2), the body of believers living by faith in the Son of God who loved them and gave Himself for them, (Galatians 2:20), children of the new Jerusalem, the Jerusalem which is above. It follows that the Galatians are children of promise, like Isaac, those who have received the blessings of Abraham and God's promise to him of justification by faith and the promise of the Holy Spirit, *all the covenantal mercies, all the covenantal blessings.*

And to carry the analogy further, just as he who was born of the flesh persecuted him who was born of the Spirit, so it is now, (Galatians 4:29). Sarah saw Ishmael playing with or laughing or mocking, (K.J.V.) her son Isaac and said to Abraham 'Cast out the slave woman and her son for the son of the slave woman shall not be heir with my son Isaac'. And the thing was very displeasing to Abraham on account of his son. But God said to Abraham, do not be displeased because of the lad and because of your slave woman. Whatever Sarah says to you, do as she tells you, for through Isaac shall your descendents be named. And I will make a nation of the son of the slave woman also, because he is your offspring'. (Genesis 21:9-13).

Though perhaps Ishmael's treatment of Isaac could hardly be called persecution, (though of course we know nothing of the details), it was certainly true of the persecution of Christians by Jews at the time of Paul, as Paul himself could testify. Paul speaks of the Thessalonian believers in his letter to them, who were in danger from their own countrymen, 'who both killed the Lord Jesus and the prophets and drove us out'. (1 Thessalonians 2:14). Paul is only saying to the Galatians what they already know, that to become a believer is to invite opposition and antagonism.

Paul returns to the original point of his analogy from Genesis 21 and Sarah's demand, 'Cast out the bondwoman and her son, for the son of the slave woman shall not inherit with the son of the free woman'. (Galatians 5:30).

This was not just the demand of a woman jealous for the inheritance of her son. This was a theological principle which Paul was stating; that there can be no compatibility, no co-existence between the law and faith. Those who are under the law and in slavery to the law are in the flesh. And those who are in the flesh cannot please God. (Romans 8:8). But those who are in the Spirit have received the Spirit of promise, the Spirit of sonship whereby we cry 'Abba! Father!' (Romans 8:15).

So brethren, Paul concludes, addressing the whole company, both men and women, (Galatians 4:28,31), we are not children of the slave woman but of the freewoman. We are brethren, brothers and sisters in Christ, and we are free. We are not children of the flesh but of the promise, the promise of the Holy Spirit. For freedom Christ has set us free. Stand fast therefore, and be not entangled again in a yoke of bondage; do not submit again to a yoke of slavery. (Galatians 5:1).

Galatians Chapter 6

Galatians 6:1-5. Love in action

> *Brethren, if anyone is overtaken in a fault, you who are spiritual should restore such a one in a spirit of gentleness. Look to yourself lest you too should be tempted. Bear one another's burdens, and so fulfil the law of Christ. (Galatians 6:1,2).*

Knowing that there will always be those among the believers who still need help as they live life in the Spirit, Paul recommends to the church ways of dealing with any who are out of the way. He says, 'Brethren', using again his affectionate word for them, 'Brethren, if someone is overtaken in a fault, a trespass, you who are spiritual, restore him or her again in a spirit of gentleness. (one of the fruits of the Spirit). Look to yourself in case you also are tempted'. (Galatians 6:1).

This is the practical application of all that Paul has been saying to them. Admittedly, the threat of heresy, of divisions in the church, the temptation to revert to slavery under the law, the need to deal with the works of the flesh; are very important issues and need to be thoroughly examined and addressed by Paul. But here is a man overtaken in a fault. We do not know what the fault is but it is serious enough for the church to need some guidance as to how to deal with him. Should we punish him? Should we excommunicate him? Cast him out from among us so that we are not defiled by his presence among us and what he has done?

No, says Paul. Restore him in a spirit of gentleness, not by rebuking him or chastising him. It is likely that his own conscience is already doing quite a good job of that. But restore him with gentleness, for there may come a time when you yourselves yield to temptation and may be in need of gentle restoration by your brothers and sisters.

Gentleness, we remember, is one of the fruits of the Spirit and is closely allied with patience and kindness. How patient God has been with us! (Romans 2:4; 1 Timothy 1:16; 1 Peter 3:20). Our hearts were hard and impenitent. We were storing up wrath for ourselves on the day of wrath when God's judgement will be revealed. But God came to us with His kindness and forbearance and patience and it was His kindness, His goodness, which led us to repentance. (Romans 2:4,5). Though we were the foremost of sinners, we received His mercy for this reason, that Christ might display His perfect patience in us, that others might receive His mercy. (1 Timothy 1:16).

And Peter reminds his readers of the patience of God, waiting, waiting for the years it took for Noah to finish building the Ark, the growing structure reminding the people of the need to seek shelter from the judgement that was coming upon the earth, but a reminder that they ignored, and perished in the flood. (1 Peter 3:20).

God is so patient, so kind towards us. He could have cast us off for our intractability when we constantly failed to listen to His call, His voice of love; for our persistent claim for self ambition, self recognition, until at last we succumbed to His urgent pleading, 'Come to Me, and I will give you rest'.

At last we found a resting place in Him and He has filled us with joy and peace in believing. (Romans 15:13). And now, in producing in us the fruit of the Spirit, He is giving us the opportunity to be loving, patient, kind towards others, a kindness which is both kind and strong for it comes from the 'Comforter', (which is etymologically a word from the Latin meaning 'with strength'), and is a hallmark of the ministry of the

Holy Spirit, the Paraclete, the One who comes alongside, the strong strengthener of followers of Jesus.

Cole, p 223, denies that Galatians 6:1-10 is just a random postscript to the letter. There is a real situation here. A man has been overtaken in a fault though we are not made aware of the details. Paul makes it clear that it is not the responsibility of the church as a whole, but of individual members to deal with this situation. Bear one another's burdens, he says, and so fulfil the law of Christ. (Galatians 6:2). What is my brother's burden? Is it the burden of guilt? Or shame? Or the inability to resist temptation? How can I care for him? How can I help him? Or perhaps, how can he help me? The possibilities appear endless. We can only approach one another in a spirit of humility, for 'when anyone thinks he is something when he is nothing, he deceives himself' (Galatians 6:3).

This is the law of Christ, the law of love, governing all that we say or do in our relationship with one another. None of us has a reason to boast and we need to test our own work to see if it comes up to the standard we have set ourselves. (Galatians 6:4). This is our burden, the burden which we ourselves carry, (Galatians 6:5), constantly alert to the needs of others, constantly alert to the promptings of the Holy Spirit.

And since we enjoy the privilege of being taught in the word by those whom our heavenly Father has set over us, we may share 'all things' with those who are teaching us. (Galatians 6:6). They carry the burden which the Holy Spirit has granted to them, the burden of teaching. We seek to make the burden lighter by our care of them, lovingly and materially.

These are the hallmarks of the Christian community. They take care of one another and especially of someone who is observed in some failure of Christian behaviour, knowing that they themselves are subject to temptation, and needing the support of others. And they not only care for one another, but for their teachers, those who faithfully instruct them in the word of God. This is the church, all heresies forgotten, all divisions healed, all living together in that love which binds everything together in perfect harmony, (Colossians 3:14), the love of Jesus, genuine love, which puts the needs of others first, even as He did.

The standard is testing one's own work, not because we hope that there is some reason to boast in one's own achievements but because a person wants to be sure that he or she is truly walking in the Spirit. He does not need to examine his neighbour's work. That is between him and his responsibility to walk in the Spirit. (Galatians 6:4). Each one of us will give account of ourselves to Christ (Romans 14:12), for the standard for each remains the same; 'bear one another's burden', but at the same time, 'each man will bear his own burden'. (Galatians 6:5).

What is Paul saying to the believers here? There is a consequence to all that a person does and he or she has to be careful not to allow themselves to be deceived. Paul writes, 'Be not deceived, God is not mocked'. You cannot deceive God. For whatsoever a man sows, tha he alo reaps. (Galatians 6:7). We cannot pretend that no such thing as deception can exist in a loving church like the one in Galatia.

In accordance with all that Paul has been writing of the difference between life lived in accordance with the flesh and life lived according to the Spirit, he now again uses the metaphor of the harvest. It is really very simple, he says. If we sow to the flesh, we shall reap to the flesh, but if we sow to the Spirit, we shall reap to the Spirit. It is a matter of cause and effect.

But sowing to the flesh brings corruption. It is only by the Holy Spirit that we can reap eternal life. And simple as it appears to be, the outcome could be very serious, for those who sow to the flesh may not only be responsible for the corruption in their own lives but may have a corrupting influence on others. Only if they sow to the Spirit will they have eternal life, the life that begins now in repentance and faith and goes on into that glorious eternity when Jesus will be glorified and they will be with Him forever. (Galatians 6:7-9).

Paul appreciates that life lived in the Spirit is not always an easy option, an easy experience. It takes the patience, the faithfulness, the generosity which have become ours as we walk in the Spirit. (Galatians 5:25). But he says, never give up. Do not grow weary in in well doing. Do not get tired of doing good for in due season you will reap if you faint not. Do not be discouraged, do not lose heart, and as you have opportunity, do good to all, especially to those who are of the household of faith. (Galatians 6:10).

For Paul, the distinction between Jew and Gentile has now gone. Now it is the distinction between those who are of the household of faith and those who have not yet responded to the gospel. Believers have a responsibility to both, to pray for them and support them in their need.

Christians were becoming known for helping each other, for example Acts 4:32-35. Those who were not Christians, but could see the way the Christians loved one another could also be drawn into the loving circle and find grace to help them in time of need. No doubt, such Christians had the hope that these others would also find the love, joy, peace which they themselves had found in Jesus. 'Let us', says Paul 'do good to all, especially to those who are of the household of faith', the loving family to which they were so content to belong. This was not a social care programme, but the spontaneous outworking of the love of Jesus in their hearts as they saw the needs of others. 'Bear one another's burdens, and so fulfil the law of Christ', says Paul. It is the only law you need. If you could only realize it, love was also the motivation for all the law given to God's people of old on Mount Sinai, God's law of love made actual and totally effective through the Lord Jesus Christ.

Perhaps, 'responsibility' expresses the thought of 'burden' more exactly for us. We have a responsibility for each other, to care for them, to help them to carry their own load whatever it might be. But we also have a personal responsibility to obey what God has given us to do, to serve Him in a way which others could not, a service unique to the individual believer, 'for each will have to carry his own load'. (Galatians 6:5).

The Lord has given to those believers whom He can trust to be obedient to Him, special responsibilities, whether it is responsibility towards others or responsibility for their own sense and conviction of what He wants them to do for Him; as if there was something that only they could do.

However heavy the load is to bear, once again they know that they can turn to the Holy Spirit, the Paraclete, the One who comes alongside; and to the Lord Jesus who gave them permission to take His yoke upon them and learn of Him, for He is meek and lowly of heart and they shall find rest to their souls. For His yoke is easy and His burden is light. (Matthew 11:28-30).

When Christians seek to bear one another's burdens, they are not attempting to interfere in another's lifestyle or moral problems, but to share with them what they have begun to rely on in their own lives, that His yoke is easy and His burden is light; to share the love of the Lord which never ceases, His mercies which never will come to an end. They are new every morning; great is His faithfulness. (Lamentations 3:22,23).

Galatians 6:11-18. Final warning and benediction

See what large letters I am writing to you with my own hand. It is those who want to make a good showing in the flesh that would compel you to be circumcised, and only that they might not be persecuted for the cross of Christ. For even those who receive circumcision do not themselves keep the law but they desire to have you circumcised that they may glory in your flesh. But far be it from me to glory except in the cross of our Lord Jesus Christ, by which the world has been crucified to me and I to the world. (Galatians 6:11-14).

Paul now comes to the conclusion of his letter. In it he has warned the Galatian believers, explained to them certain truths, encouraged them, and above all, reassured them of his love for them. He has defined for them how they may personally live in the Spirit and how collectively they may live as the family of God.

Though his conclusive words sum up most of what he has been saying to them, it is still a strongly worded attempt to 'keep the main thing as the main thing', (Dr R.T Kendall), the main thing being justification by faith alone through Christ alone, living in the freedom whereby God has made men and women free; life in the Spirit as sons and daughters, not slaves but heirs.

The whole impetus of the writing of this letter by Paul has been to expose their fragility as those newly come to Christ, and the seriousness of listening to those false teachers who would bring them into bondage, the bondage from which they had been delivered, released, when they turned to Christ. (Galatians 1:6).

In these closing words, Paul opposes two concepts to them. To engage with circumcision so they are not persecuted, on the one hand, or with the cross of Christ on the other. Paul refers to what they already know by this time, that the cross of Christ, when applied to their lives, is a completely different instrument, bringing them into increasing fellowship with Him and the Holy Spirit, enabling them to call God, 'Father' as they enter into sonship.

Paul emphasises the importance of the last words he is writing to them by drawing attention once again to his poor eyesight, as he had in Galatians 4:5, and therefore of the need to employ an amanuensis. But how Paul longed after them in the truth, laying these ultimate truths before then in his own handwriting as proof of his pastoral care for them. This was a physical problem which might have interfered with their receiving of the gospel, but far from making his preaching unacceptable, it actually helped, through their compassion towards him. In fact, they received him as an angel of God, as Christ Jesus. (Galatians 4:14).

This reminder of the relationship into which Paul and the Galatians had entered was given by Paul to show them how greatly he understood their dilemma. Circumcision was like a passport. If someone was circumcised it would save him from persecution by the Jews who wanted him to keep the law; it would save him from persecution from the Romans who recognized Judaism as a religion and in some though not all administrations allowed them to practise it.

Circumcision was such a small and insignificant ritual to be observed and it had all these advantages. Why not therefore be circumcised? This was the argument of the troublemakers of Galatians 2:4. Paul sees it for what it is. It is the alternative to living life in the glory of the cross of Christ, for those who are trying to compel the believers to be circumcised are wanting to glory in their flesh, both that flesh which constitutes their bodily form, but also that inner part of themselves which has been set free by the cross, their spirit (Galatians 6:14). Paul says, far be it from me to glory save in the cross of our Lord Jesus Christ.

The cross of Christ was shameful, humiliating, unspeakably horrific. It was understandable that the early Christians would not necessarily want to admit how important the cross was to them. Indeed, Paul admits that the very word of the cross was a scandal to Jews and foolishness to the Greeks. (1 Corinthians 1:18).

But he also responds with all his heart to the sublime knowledge that the cross is the power of God unto salvation. (Romans 1:16). By no other means could his life have been transformed. By the cross, the world had been crucified to him and he to the world. (Galatians 6:14). By the cross, he measures everything else and finds it wanting. There is nothing in the world which attracts him, wealth, possessions, power, influence. To him, the cross is everything; the place where God is revealed in Christ in all His glorious mercy and concern for fallen, sinful men and women.

In the light of the cross, neither circumcision nor uncircumcision counts for anything. Both are totally irrelevant. What does matter is a new creation, a new creature, utterly different, utterly transformed (Galatians 6:15). And if anyone is in Christ, *he is a new creature. The old has passed, the new has come.* (2 Corinthians 5:17). No wonder Paul can say to these Galatian believers 'Peace be upon all who walk by this rule and upon the Israel of God'. God did so much for His people, the people of Israel before Christ came, under the Old Covenant. But He has a new creation in Christ, who are living not under the Old Covenant, but under the New Covenant in His blood, (Luke 22:20); the new Israel.

So Paul's final words to his beloved Galatians is, 'Henceforth, let no one trouble me for I bear in my body the marks of Jesus'. (Galatians 6:17). What Paul calls the marks of Jesus can be regarded as stigmata, a constant reminder to Paul that he is a slave of Jesus. Stigmata were very offensive for slaves were branded or tattooed to certify that they were the property of their owners, especially if they had been runaway slaves.

In contrast to the marks of circumcision, Paul carried the marks of Jesus. He says, 'I am a marked man, I am stigmatized, branded'. This may refer to the many injuries he had received, his suffering for the Lord as he preached His word, for example the stoning he received at Lystra (Acts 14:9), the beating he and Barnabas received in the prison at Philippi, (Acts 16: 22,23), or later, from the fetters and chains he wore when in prison. (Acts 26:29).

But these marks only served to draw him closer still to the Lord Jesus and His grace. He knew himself to be surrounded, embraced by that grace, and if his Galatian brothers and sisters remembered nothing else of all that he had written to them, he wanted them to remember this, that together they shared the love and grace of God; His undeserved love and favour towards them.

He writes 'the grace of our Lord Jesus Christ be with your spirit, my brothers and sisters. Amen'. (Galatians 6:18). They cannot have enough of the grace of the Lord Jesus. Paul began with grace at the beginning of this letter to them and grace is at the end. (Galatians 1:3). When this letter was read out to them, the Galatians would surely have echoed Paul's 'Amen'.

Select Bibliography

Barclay, William, *The Letter to the Galatians and Ephesians,* (Edinburgh: The Saint Andrew Press, 1958)

Bruce, F.F., *The Epistle to the Galatians,* (Michigan: Wm.B. Eerdmans Publishing Company, 1982)

Cole, R. Alan, *Galatians,* (Michigan: Wm.B. Eerdmans Publishing Company, 1999)

Dunn, James D.G., *The Theology of Paul's Letter to the Galatians,* (Cambridge: Cambridge University Press, 1993)

Esler, Philip F., *Galatians*, (Oxford, Routledge, 1998)

Kung, Ronald Y.K., *The Epistle to the Galatians*, (Michigan, Wm.B. Eerdmans Publishing Company, 1998)

Stott, John, *The Message of Galatians*, (Westmont, IL, Inter-Varsity Press, 2020)

www.ingramcontent.com/pod-product-compliance
Lightning Source LLC
LaVergne TN
LVHW041253080426
835510LV00009B/721